A UNIVERSE BEYOND PERFECTION

"This is the room I dreamed of," Treaia said in a hushed voice.

Mey nodded in agreement, as he looked upward to a ceiling of majestic height. On the east wall, facing them, was an altar with fingers of golden light beaming down on a living flame that burned brightly from the center. Gazing at the flame, Mey and Treaia began to feel dizzy. Their heads started spinning with the astonishing beauty they had found, and this spinning caused them to step out of their physical bodies. Now they could see each other as they truly were—pure love. Looking at each other, they stepped toward one another and blended, becoming one.

Once upon no time,
way off beyond imagination,
stands a land called Everfor . . .

The
PLANET
of
TEARS

Trish Reinius

Illustrations
by
Bob Johnson

BANTAM BOOKS
Toronto / New York / London

This low-priced Bantam Book
has been completely reset in a type face
designed for easy reading, and was printed
from new plates. It contains the complete
text of the original hard-cover edition.
NOT ONE WORD HAS BEEN OMITTED.

THE PLANET OF TEARS
A Bantam Book / published by arrangement with
Dawne-Leigh Publications

PRINTING HISTORY
Dawne-Leigh edition published May 1979
Bantam edition / December 1980

Book designed by Cathy Marinaccio

ISBN 0-553-13996-7

Published simultaneously in the United States and Canada

PRINTED IN THE UNITED STATES OF AMERICA

0 9 8 7 6 5 4 3 2 1

Dedicated to my Darling Angels
Tonie, Jenifer Ann, Maureen, and
Jenifer's Grandpa

Contents

Chapter One

Everfor

Once upon no time, way off beyond imagination, stands a land called Everfor. This land, and we must call it a land because we know no other term for it, is a part of our universe; but we cannot see it with telescopes—not because of distance but because of dimension. Everfor is not composed of substance; you might say it is invisible. But it is very real although it is unseen, as are many things in this universe. Everfor stretches out beyond darkness, for all is light and golden there.

In Everfor is a city of great domes and spirals rising to grand peaks, where all the buildings are white and gold, tipped with an edge of silver. The white is a white of brilliant light, like a star far off in the distance, and the gold and silver sparkle so exquisitely that each tiny particle seems to emit its own radiance. Rainbows stream out from every direction, making the sky look like mother-of-pearl. Music seems to come from everywhere and nowhere—music like the twinkling of all the stars in the heavens, or like brilliant suns bursting forth.

Throughout Everfor there are gardens arranged in the perfection of the universe, for disorder is unknown there. The trees bear blossoms of unusual design; and flowers bloom in every shape and color. Some even have stems of gold and petals of diamonds, which glitter and change color as the light hits them. The rainbows in Everfor serve a very special purpose—in fact more than one. (For there is more than one kind of rainbow, you know.) Some serve as bridges between one part of Everfor and another, and when the citizens of Everfor step on such a rainbow, it transports them gently but swiftly to their destination.

Now let us go back many thousands of years to the time of our story, when the planets were very different, but Everfor was the same as it is now and always will be. Long, long ago two beautiful beings of Everfor were riding on a rainbow bridge. They were wearing robes of a white iridescent fabric that glowed with every color in Everfor; their hair was long and golden; and their faces were so beautiful that they seemed to radiate, from within their bodies, every wonderful thing that had ever been. Although they were two, sometimes they seemed to merge into one. Their names were Mey and Treaia.

Mey and Treaia were on their way to the grand council chamber in the city of domes and spirals, where they had been called for a very important reason. The council chamber was a large, round room high up in the tallest dome of the city, and in the center of the chamber stood the supreme ruler of Everfor, Melkedek. How magnificent he looked! He was as beautiful as Mey and Treaia, but his eyes shone with still greater depths of wisdom and love. Seven others stood around him, similar in appearance. Melkedek wore a shining white robe trimmed in gold and silver, and the seven others each wore a different colored robe, spanning the whole range from red to violet, so that all the glorious colors of the rainbow were represented.

The council room was surrounded with large mirrors that looked like windows, in each of which appeared a scene from a different world. As Mey and Treaia entered the room, they saw the members of the council gazing with deep absorption into one of these mirrors. Mey and Treaia bowed low to Melkedek and to the others.

Then Melkedek spoke, and his voice echoed from heart to heart in the chamber, "Come, Mey and Treaia, and look at the Planet of Tears with us, for that is the world we have been watching. We have sent for you to tell you this: the time has come for you to go to one of the planets, to continue your journey on the path of existence. Like all the other beings of Everfor, you have journeyed from Everfor many times before, and each time you have gone to one of the planets to continue to learn the lessons of life. Now the Planet of Tears is entering the Age of Aries and as you know, this will be a particularly evil time. It will be a time of trials, and perhaps your struggle will be hard and long. But it will also be a time of opportunity, since the chance for the greatest progress lies in the sharpest struggle. It is time for you to go. Know that you are loved and that you are special, as all beings are special."

Then Melkedek shone his light on them and said kindly, "We will send you over a rainbow bridge and you will each descend in a golden spiral to your separate destinations. Since you will be in different locations, you will be able to progress to new knowledge in a shorter time than if you were together. You see, if you started out together, you would be so satisfied with having each other that you would not seek out the ways of the beings on the Planet of Tears. And it will be necessary for you to learn about their ways in order to learn more about yourselves.

"You will take on a dense physical form, made up of the elements of their planet, and you will have no memory of Everfor, except perhaps for an occasional dream.

"You cannot really lose the love and knowledge that are within you, but you will have to learn how to use their qualities on the Planet of Tears. You will be like the other inhabitants of the planet, except of course that all will be at different stages on the path of existence, and you must get by on your own merits and decisions when you face the trials and tests of the planet. You will be put into environments that will give you the opportunity to learn," Melkedek continued in his deep voice, "and it will be up to you to use those opportunities. Perhaps, if you are successful, you will reach a point where you can be of service to the planet. That will be your highest goal and aspiration. But remember that when you take on physical form, there are many ways to become detoured and entrapped. So beware!

"You must conquer individually, and then together you must also conquer. If you fail to find one another, there is a danger that you could be trapped on the Planet of Tears, and spend a millenium recycling life after life, accomplishing nothing. Also remember that desire is a very strong force on that sphere, and is a force you will surely have to reckon with.

"You must strive to become in the physical world what you are here. This is the mission of all beings sent from Everfor, but it is a difficult task. It is very hard to bring eternal qualities into the physical existence, and the dangers are many. If you succeed, know that you will return to Everfor with a quality you do not now possess. This quality will enable you to go to even greater heights than Everfor."

Then Mey and Treaia sighed, although they knew

that they must go. "Mighty Melkedek," they said, "we shall be so far away and we shall not be able to ask your advice and help. We shall be so alone."

But Melkedek answered them with a smile, "Remember that from time to time you can cross the rainbow bridge to Everfor. Of course you will not take your forms from the Planet of Tears. You will leave them in the care of sleep while you visit here. You will not always remember all of your visit, but it will be there within your being when you need it.

"In the past, when you have journeyed across the rainbow bridge to the world of the planets, you have dealt well with the struggles and hardships of life in the physical form. Each time you go back, therefore, your level of knowledge and love is greater than the last time. On the journey on which you are about to embark, you will find that you will be two of the most highly evolved beings on the planet, but do not be afraid of being alone. Other beings from Everfor will be there to help. Each has a different task to accomplish. A few have never changed form during the greater cycle they are spending there. Most follow the normal cycle of that planet and return to Everfor from time to time until their task is finished and the greater cycle is completed. You will follow the latter plan."

Mey and Treaia smiled and were reassured.

"One more thing before you must go," Melkedek said, as he again put his light around Mey and Treaia. "Many of the creatures on the Planet of Tears can be helpful to you. In fact most of nature on that planet is helpful, if you are alert to its ways. Now come," he said, taking their hands, "I will lead you across the rainbow bridge and send you down the spirals."

Chapter Two

Treaia

Standing with outstretched arms, making a salutation to the sun as it rose upon the horizon, stood the high priestess of the temple, Ramana. She was a mature woman of exceptional stature, slender of form. Her hair looked dark until the first light of the rising sun shone on it, turning it a blazing copper. Her eyes were almond-shaped and the color of emeralds, her skin a delicate gold. It was hard to tell her age, because she was well cared for. The temple steps were deeply worn; they had been there for a long, long time. The temple was very ancient, and the form of worship conducted there was so old that there was no memory or record of its origin. The only thing left from the earliest days of its mysteries were certain jewels, symbols of the wisdom and authority of these mysteries. The care of the jewels was the sacred task of Ramana.

Ramana gazed out at the eastern sea, toward which the temple faced. Then her gaze turned toward the meadow and the temple's orchards. Ramana was admiring the new blossoms on the fruit trees when she suddenly noticed a strange thing—a wispy, golden, spiraling whirlwind, accompanied by strains of music so soft that she could barely hear it. She watched as the whirlwind disappeared, wondering what it could have been.

"It must have been my imagination," she said to herself, as she started to go inside the temple. But just then she heard the faint sounds of a child. Straining her eyes and ears to find out where the sounds were coming from, she saw that in the spot where she had seen the golden whirlwind lay a tiny child. She ran over quickly with her long measured stride.

When Ramana reached the child, she knew immediately that she had never seen a more beautiful girl child in all her life—her skin was like ivory, her hair like the raven's. But oh, to look into her eyes, they were a blue-violet, and seemed to contain the depths of the universe. "Wherever did you come from?" exclaimed Ramana in awe. But the little girl was not old enough to speak and only smiled at her sweetly.

Ramana picked her up carefully and took her into the temple, causing a stir of excitement among the temple helpers, who represented all the many different types of people living in this land. Their skin tones and hair varied from fair to the deepest black, but none looked like Ramana or the little child who had just arrived. It was the custom in this land for every village to send one or two youths, upon reaching puberty, to serve the gods. Most of them were content to work and live at the temple, for the high priestess was fair and just. She tried to see that their needs were met, and the few who wanted to learn the real truths, she taught.

"Worthy priestess, we have had no travelers or visitors here for some time," said one of the helpers. "How could this child have come here?" (The temple was far away from any town or village.)

"Where *did* she come from?" Ramana thought, as she stood with the child still in her arms. "Perhaps the strange golden whirlwind brought her here. I wonder if it could be so. I myself was brought here when I was very young to be trained for the position of high priestess, and yet I still do not know from where."

These and many other thoughts quickly ran through Ramana's mind, and finally she answered the helper, "I do not know where she came from. When I perform the nightly ritual, I will ask for an answer."

Since she was one of the more advanced beings of the land and trained as the high priestess of the temple, Ramana had more knowledge than anyone else, which also gave her powers of insight into unknown things. That night, during the ritual, she had a vision that spoke to her, saying, "My daughter, this child was brought to you for the purpose of raising her and teaching her all that you know. Name her Treaia, for it will make her happy and she will feel less alone."

So the next day Ramana told her helpers that the child was a gift from the gods, and that she intended to raise her to become the next high priestess. Then she took her out into the garden and sat down on the bench with the child on her lap. "You are to be my daughter," she said gently, "and I am to name you Treaia." Just then a beautiful little bird fluttered by and the child started laughing in delight. Her blue-violet eyes had sparkles of gold dashing from them. "Oh little one, you do like the name," said Ramana when she saw the child laugh. "So it shall be. You are to be called Treaia."

Now the people at the temple were not used to having a small child about the place, for there was no one who could remember when Ramana had come, and so Treaia became the delight of all as she was growing up. As the years went by, Ramana taught everything she knew to Treaia. And Treaia taught something to Ramana; that something was to love another fully and completely. For despite all her knowledge Ramana had never learned to love until she became Treaia's mother.

Treaia grew into a beautiful but restless young girl. Her life was full of discipline and learning, and sometimes it seemed to her as if everything that existed was run by the sound of the temple gong—time to get up, time to say prayers, time to eat, time to study, and time to go to bed. Treaia began to feel that her whole life throbbed to the ringing of the gong, and she began to hate the gong. Every time it rang she would make an ugly face, hoping against hope that somehow it would never ring again.

One day Treaia decided she wanted to get rid of the gong, but when she tried it was much too large and much too heavy for her to handle. She sat and looked at it for a long time, telling it how much she loathed it, but then she had a marvelous idea. She would ring it herself, only not at the usual times. So she waited until everyone was in bed asleep, and she stole down and struck the gong three times. Then she ran away and hid and had a wonderful time watching all the excitement and scurrying around. She was only nine years old, so this gave her a tremendous feeling of power over the hated gong. But after several weeks Ramana finally caught her in the act, and her control over the gong was ended.

The older Treaia became, the more rebellious she grew, until sometimes, when the gong rang, she refused to go to the temple for the ceremonies or to her studies, but instead she would run off to the beach or to the fields, talking to the birds and small animals. Treaia loved the life in all things, from the tiniest insect to every rock on the shores of the sea. The creatures and objects of nature were her friends and her only playmates. Because of her loving nature, it was always hard for Ramana to punish her when she finally came back, which she always did, for there was nowhere else to go.

Ramana knew how lonely Treaia was at times, and so she allowed her to share the company of any travelers who stopped to visit the temple. Treaia loved to hear stories of grand palaces and of parties where young people laughed and played games. But these stories only made her more restless, sometimes even resentful. She wanted more out of life than to grow up and be the next high priestess.

But Treaia loved Ramana and the temple helpers. Sometimes she even enjoyed studying and learning. The temple helpers always asked her advice if they had a problem, and she would sit in interested silence until sooner or later they would answer their own questions. Many would come to have her make them laugh when they were sad. Treaia was glad if she could help, but she always wished she had a friend of her own to make *her* laugh, someone to share adventures with.

Sometimes Treaia woke up at night with strange dreams, and she told them to Ramana. "Dearest mother, if only I could remember all of my dreams instead of only parts," she would say. "I'm left with such vague feelings. It seems as if I should remember something important."

"It doesn't matter if you don't remember your dreams, little one, if you always listen to the gentle tugs of your inner self when you must make a decision," Ramana told her.

So Treaia took Ramana's hand in hers and, taking a deep breath, started to blurt out all her pent-up feelings. "I don't want to be the high priestess, dear Ramana. Please let us move to a city or a town and live like the people we have heard stories about. Let's have fun, let's play and have parties and wear pretty clothes. Oh mother, don't you see how happy we both could be!"

Gently Ramana put her arms around Treaia, and as she spoke her voice began to quiver. "My child, I know how you feel. At one time I too was very lonely here. You were chosen to fulfill the position of high priestess, just as I was chosen a long time ago. You must resign yourself to your fate or you will never be content here, as the rest of us are. You must discipline yourself, and begin to perform your duties. Now that you are older, you must not be disobedient any longer. After I am gone you will have to attend to all the duties that this high office requires. You can never let the others know you have any weaknesses."

"But mother," Treaia started to say, as tears rolled down her cheeks.

"No, daughter, do not speak of it any more. It is your fate, and you must accept it," Ramana said in a firm voice. "Go back to bed now. Your unhappiness will pass away, as all things do."

Treaia never again spoke to Ramana of leaving, because she knew Ramana's decision was firm. She could not leave without her mother for she loved her, and who would watch over her if she went without Ramana? So she tried harder to be obedient and to do her duties with cheerfulness.

The temple was a pleasant place to live, and Treaia tried to think of how lucky she was to have such a nice home and good people around her, people who loved her and cared for her. She tried hard to push away her restless thoughts, but somehow they always crept back into her head. They were so exciting.

"Maybe God will help me to find a way to live the life I want," she thought to herself, "if only I were sure just *what* I really want. I know I want to do exciting things and have fun like the people I've heard about, and not live by the sound of a gong, but what I want to do instead, I'm not at all sure."

So Treaia prayed, but she was never quite sure what to ask for, except that life shouldn't be quite so dull and that she wouldn't have to be the high priestess. These uncertain and changing prayers she never spoke aloud, and when she finished them, she would continue softly, "Oh God, help me to be obedient and content to fulfill my ordained duties. Help me to make my mother proud of me," and with a sigh, she would rise from her prayers and try very hard, at least until the next time she could not resist the urge to ignore the gong.

One exceptionally beautiful morning, Treaia ignored

the sound of the gong and walked down to the beach. Once she was by the water and running along the sand, she felt happy, finding pleasure in all the small shells, looking into the tidepools, and marveling at the sea urchins. It felt so good and she was so happy to be alive. Today everything was wonderful here in the world she lived in. As she was looking at a shell, a ray of sunshine hit the mother-of-pearl in the shell, revealing its rainbow of colors and causing a strange warm feeling to well up in her heart. "Little shell of many colors, somehow you make me feel different inside my heart. Whisper to me and tell me your secret," Treaia pleaded.

Suddenly, faint but violent sounds came to Treaia's ears. As she listened, she thought she could hear the sound of screaming coming from far away, from the direction of the temple. In great anxiety, she got up and started back, and the closer she got, the louder the sounds became. Her heart pounding, she started to run, and when the temple came into view she was astonished to see strange-looking boats bobbing in the water, and men hurriedly loading objects into them. Then she saw smoke and flames swirling up from the temple. Treaia felt fear in her heart for the first time, as she ran on in terror, yelling, "Ramana, Ramana, what is it? What has happened?"

As Treaia entered the temple gates she began to cry and sob hysterically. There, lying on the ground and on the steps, with spears in their bodies, were the temple helpers. The temple had been destroyed by fire, and all the beautiful art objects that had adorned the temple were gone, leaving a picture of desolation and horror. Treaia had never seen death or destruction before, and the ugliness of it was almost too much for her to bear. Then, as she stood weeping at the sight, she heard Ramana's voice faintly off in the distance. "Ramana! Where are you? Oh mother, I thought you were gone, I thought I was left alone," Treaia called, trying to follow Ramana's faint voice. Finally she found her mother in a corner of the garden, hiding behind a bush and clutching a small bag to her breast. In relief, Treaia ran to her, crying, "Oh thank the gods you're all right! Oh, Ramana,

tell me what has happened here to our beautiful temple
and all our people."

Ramana hushed Treaia, whispering in a weak voice,
"We haven't much time, Treaia, so listen to me carefully
now. I have been the keeper of the jewels since they were
passed on to me when I became high priestess. They
hold the secret of all knowledge and wisdom, but the
secret was forgotten so long ago that I cannot tell you
what it is. Last night in the temple I had a vision that
someone would come to steal the jewels, to take to an
evil man, but I thought I was mistaken, because it has
been peaceful here for as long as I can remember. Then
when the looters and murderers came upon us I was in
the temple. A spear hit me; but I managed to snatch up
the jewels and hide here in the garden, praying you were
kept safe. For once I was glad you had disobeyed."

It was then that Treaia saw the blood seeping
through Ramana's garments. The tears welling up in her
eyes again, Treaia sobbed, "Please don't leave me, my
mother! Without you my heart will surely break!"

"Wait, child, I am an old woman now. It would soon
have been time for me to leave you even if this had not
happened. And it would have been time to pass on to you
the keeping of the jewels," whispered Ramana.

"But Ramana, how can I keep the jewels with no
temple to put them in?" said Treaia, still sobbing.

Ramana was growing weak and was barely able to
whisper to Treaia, "You, my daughter, are the temple of
the jewels. And in the vision I had last night, I was told
there is a missing part to the secret. You must leave this
place and start journeying to find it." Then, with these
words, Ramana breathed her last breath; her spirit left her
body for another place.

"Forgive me, mother, for not obeying you," cried
Treaia. "Please don't leave me. I'm sorry I prayed for my
life to change. Please make things like they were before.
Please, mother, I'll do as you say, only don't leave me."
Treaia held Ramana in her arms and begged her, but
Ramana could no longer hear.

Treaia was pulled gently away from Ramana by two
temple helpers who had hidden in the orchard when the

raiders had come. "It's no use, young priestess, she is dead. All are dead but the three of us," said one of them.

Never let your weakness show, Ramana had once told Treaia. So, wiping her eyes on her tunic, she said to them, "We must tend to the dead and after that you are free to go where you like. Ramana told me that I was to go on a journey to find a secret."

And after everything was done that could be done, Treaia said goodbye to the two helpers. "Why did I ever want anything different? Forgive me," whispered Treaia, and, taking one last look at the only world she had ever known, she took her first step alone, though into what she did not know.

Chapter Three

Treaia Wanders

A white tunic belted with a cordilier and a bag of jewels tied to her waist were all the possessions left to Treaia as she reluctantly started on her journey. Her feet were bare, for she had left her sandals in the temple while she had been on the beach, and they too had been consumed by the ugly flames. The wind blew her long hair and she raised her hand to push it back from her eyes, a look of sadness and shock on her young face. She was not quite so young inside any more after this day.

Evening shadows were already creeping over the land as she headed in the direction of the nearest village. Treaia had met an old man from this village many years ago, when he had brought a youth to the temple to serve the gods. Generally, the temple helpers had told her stories about how the people of the land lived, and about the homes they had lived in before they had been chosen to come to the temple to serve the gods. But the helper from this nearest village had been different. He had been silent, withdrawn, and uncommunicative. Treaia wondered what kind of reception she was going to be given in the village that lay ahead.

Walking during the day and sleeping at night, she made her way onward in a state of shock. In her dazed condition she did not notice her hunger or the many blisters on her feet. That horrible day had brought her many experiences she had never known—fear, destruction, loss, and guilt—and it was hard for her to learn to cope with these ugly and frightening feelings.

But shock helped to numb the horror of the terrible destruction and loss, and fear of the unknown had not yet had time to seep into her being. However, her heart was full of guilt. Treaia muttered incoherently to herself as she stumbled along, "Did *I* cause the destruction, by my prayers? I never meant for anything to happen to Ramana and the others—you know that, don't you, Ramana? Dear God, I didn't mean it that way. I didn't do it, it was those men, but would they have come if I hadn't been praying for something different? I won't have to be the high priestess now. I'm sorry, oh Ramana, what will I do now? Mother, mother, I miss you, I need you."

As time passed and as she walked, her thoughts of Ramana took her back to one of the many times they had talked in the garden. "Dear Ramana," Treaia had said, "through the years you have taught me much. Today tell me more about the world and the people who live in it, for I know nothing but the way of life we have here."

Ramana had sighed and remained silent a moment or two; then she had spoken with a strange sadness. "Treaia, you, I and a few of the helpers believe in one God, although we see him acting in many ways. So sometimes we speak of many gods. Most of the people of this land believe in many gods, some good and some evil. They blame everything on the gods and accept no responsibility for their own acts. They cannot forget their own selfishness and greed long enough to learn and understand the workings of God's laws and they learn slowly through bitter experience. At a certain stage of existence this is the only way men can learn, and many more stages of existence must pass before they will learn to understand and reason. Then they will learn easily how to treat one another with kindness. But do not despair, Treaia," Ramana said, as she saw a look of concern come into Treaia's eyes. "The high priestess before me told me that there are other more evolved beings in this world, though not very many."

"How sad, Ramana, that everyone does not want to learn all the wonderful things that are just waiting for us to find," Treaia had sighed.

"No, child, very few are as we are. You came here to me with an ability to love and find joy in all living things that some of us did not have. You didn't have to learn to love as I did. So I have learned from you, as you have learned from me. Knowledge is not powerful without love to wield it, Treaia. Although you are young and sometimes disobedient, you have the gift of love."

"Why is it that we from the temple do not go to the villages and teach the people, so they can know the truths?" Treaia had asked.

"It has been tried before," said Ramana. "But it was found that unless a person wants to learn, you cannot teach him, just as when you ignore the gong," Ramana smiled. "It is better for people to seek their own source of learning; then they are receptive to new things, and that is one of the reasons why we are so far away. Even so, very few of the ones who have journeyed here have stayed to learn. They want us to tell them what to do, to pray for them, and they never want to learn to do things for themselves. Ignorance is the greatest danger in the land. But teaching someone is a slow process, until he wants to know."

Barking dogs brought Treaia back from her thoughts, and she found herself at the edge of the village. So, taking a deep breath, she walked in and looked around her cautiously. Immediately she realized that it was a very primitive place; there were no houses, just huts built out of the native river grass. Although it was a picturesque village with flowers and trees growing among the huts, nothing seemed to have been planted by the people; all the vegetation appeared to be natural growth. There was a large stone altar, around which Treaia thought they must hold their rituals to the gods. She saw a fire was burning in the middle of a clearing between the huts, where an old woman was cooking in a large black pot.

Finally she heard a shout and realized that someone had noticed her. The people slowly came out of their huts, and a crowd gathered to stare at her. They began to whisper among themselves and pointed their long dark fingers. Treaia felt very frightened, until she saw a dried-up, withered old man approaching her, whom she recognized as the old man who had brought the youth to the temple many years before. How relieved she was to see him!

"Priestess, why are you here and not at your temple many days away?" the old man's voice crackled.

"Our temple was burned and looted; and I am one of only three survivors. I must journey to find the secret of the jewels. Can you help me?" asked Treaia.

"Why did your gods not protect you? Did the high priestess and yourself lose the power to control the gods?" the old man continued to question.

"Now I see what Ramana meant when she told me that some people prefer to be ignorant," thought Treaia. "This man has been to the temple and he has been told that we do not control the gods. Yet he insists on keeping his superstitious belief." Realizing how primitive these people were, Treaia became very afraid. "I must say something to protect myself," she thought.

"Worthy old man," spoke Treaia, "it was time for the great high priestess Ramana to leave this land and go with the gods. This was the gods' work, so that she might be free to leave the temple. I was spared so that I might make a journey to search for a secret."

Easily the old man understood that this was the working of the gods, so he spoke again, "I will hold a meeting and talk to my people to see what they want to do with you. Wait here; food and water will be brought to you." He smiled a toothless grin as he walked away.

Relieved for the moment but quite exhausted, Treaia sat down under a tree and leaned back against it, closing her eyes. Presently someone nudged her, and she looked up to see a young girl holding a bowl of food in one hand and a bowl of water in the other. Treaia smiled at the girl and said, "Thank you, I'm very tired and hungry after my long walk. Won't you sit down and talk to me while I eat?"

But the young girl only stared at her, open-mouthed. Except for the old man, no one in this village had ever seen anyone who looked like Treaia.

Treaia tried again to talk to the girl, "Please won't you tell me your name?" But the girl shoved the bowls into Treaia's hands and ran away. When the girl was some distance away, she turned and looked. "How strange to have someone run from me," thought Treaia, as she ate the food in the bowl. "Even stranger is the taste of this food. I wonder if I am eating an animal? We never ate meat at the temple. Ramana told me that most people in the world do so; and that it is not bad if you give thanks for the use of the animal's body, and if it was not killed in terror."

The moon was up and glowing pleasantly in the night sky when the old man returned, saying, "I have told my people that you are a priestess from the far-off temple, and that you have powers that enable you to speak with the gods. You may stay here in our village. We will give you a hut and food and in return you will speak to the gods for us."

"When you visited our temple were you not told that

you, yourself, could talk to the god of all things?" Treaia asked the old man.

"Yes, I was told this. But we believe that only children of the gods can do so—like you, the chosen one of the temple," said the old man, frowning.

"Ramana was right again in saying that some people will not accept knowledge," thought Treaia, as she looked deep into the elder's eyes.

"Old man, I will accept your kind offer to stay here for a while, since I do not know where else to go. I will pray to the gods for you and your people," Treaia said in acceptance.

Each morning and evening the same girl who had first brought her something to eat put two bowls at the opening of her hut, one of food, the other of water. Treaia never knew what would be in her food bowl, for these people existed on their ability to hunt and find grains and fruits where they grew wild. They did no cultivating of their own. Her hut was at the farthest end of the village, away from the rest of the huts, and the people feared her because she was different. She not only looked different, but she could talk to the gods. To them she was powerful; and power was to be feared.

Treaia sat in her hut and brooded about her circumstances. Sometimes she felt she deserved her present condition because of her dissatisfaction with her life at the temple. At other times she hated being in the village and would throw herself down on the floor of the hut and sob until she slept. She was afraid to do anything. Where could she go? These people were so ignorant that they couldn't tell her anything, even if they wanted to. But at least for the time being she had a place to sleep and food to eat. And all she had to do was talk to the gods!

One day the weather became humid and the heat almost unbearable, for the village was far from the sea. With the humid air came a horde of flying biting insects. When the people became sick from the bites, the old man came to see Treaia. He bowed to her and said, "Priestess, it is time for you to speak to the gods and make these demons go away. Can you not see that they are making my people sick?"

"I will do what I can," answered Treaia. She looked around to see what kinds of trees and herbs there might be in the vicinity, for she was trained in the ways of healing.

"See that tall tree, the one with the long thin leaves," she said to the old man. "Have some of your men fetch a pot full of the leaves and drain some of the sap that runs inside the tree."

The old man scurried off and did as he was bid. After the task was completed he returned to Treaia, saying, "We have the big cooking pot full of the leaves and sap that you asked for."

Treaia's heart pounded fiercely. Knowing she must let these people think the gods were responsible, she made her way to the center of the village where the large black pot stood. "Put the pot on the fire spot," commanded Treaia. The old man had the pot lifted onto the fire. With that Treaia raised her hands to the sky, singing songs that she had sung in the temple, and walking around and around the pot. As the pot began to heat up, the sap started to melt, releasing the fragrance of the sap and leaves throughout the village. It was a fresh clean smell. As the odor went out, the insects started to disappear, and seeing this, all the people bowed down to her. Treaia said to them, "If you wish to keep insects away, keep a pot of these leaves and sap burning at all times. That is what the gods have told me." The old man thanked her and led her back to her hut.

Each morning and evening when the girl brought the bowls, Treaia would speak to her, hoping to make a friend. But each day the girl quickly put the bowls down and ran. Treaia had hoped that after helping them with the insects they would be more friendly to her, but no. She was very lonely and unhappy. She needed a friend, someone to share her sorrows with, but not one would speak to her; even the young girl rejected her. After some days of this, Treaia searched out the old man, since no one else would talk to her. Sadly she asked him, "Kindly talk to me, old man. Tell me why your people avoid me, and worse yet, run from me when I wish to be friends?"

"Do you not know that no one here can talk to you because you are a priestess? If they should happen to talk to you the gods will be angry with them," answered the old man solemnly.

"Why is it then that you talk to me?" asked Treaia.

"That is different. I am the chief here, and worthy," the old man said with pride.

So the days passed in loneliness. Each day she prayed to the one god of gods to send the people of the village understanding, the very thing they resisted. But in her loneliness she began to remember her dreams more often. One night she dreamed of a handsome prince with a sword in his hand, who looked at her with more love than she had ever seen, and she felt this same love back for him. In her waking moments, she would often think of this prince of her dreams, and she began to hope every day that someone would find her and take care of her. Then she would think of Ramana and know that soon she would have to seek after the secret of the jewels.

On arising one morning, Treaia left her hut to greet the new day, as was her custom, and when she looked to the sky, there was the darkest storm cloud she had ever seen. "I have never seen clouds like that before, moving with such force," she said to herself as she gazed upward.

"The god of storms is coming to get us," screamed the villagers, who began to gather up their belongings and run. But it was too late. The winds started ripping off the roofs and throwing the huts up into the air, and with the wind came a sleeting rain that blew in every direction.

Her tunic and hair blowing wildly in the wind, Treaia stood and stared in disbelief. Her hut was blown right out from behind her, and then she was thrown against a tree, so she grabbed hold of the tree and hung on. Now the wind was so fierce that anything loose was thrown high up in the air and cast down, mangled, far away. She clung to the tree with all her strength and prayed. "God, please make me strong enough to hang on," whispered Treaia, for the sounds were awful to hear. The howling of the wind and rain was mixed with the terrified cries of the villagers.

Suddenly there was silence; the storm had passed. It seemed to leave as it had come, quickly and unexpectedly. Treaia lay against the tree, exhausted. The villagers were sobbing, looking perplexed, and they seemed to be

in a state of delirium as they tried to gather up what was
left of their homes. Then suddenly someone yelled,
"Grab her, she is evil, she has no power." Soon others
joined in, saying, "It is her fault that the god of storms
came, her prayers are no good." With this all the villagers
descended on Treaia en masse. "Sacrifice, sacrifice,"
screamed the mob of frightened angry people.

"You don't understand. It is not my fault that the
storm came," yelled Treaia in terror, as she saw the hate
and fear on their faces. She shrank back, but they pushed
her one way and pulled her the other until she felt as
though she was being pulled in half. "Help, someone,
help," she screamed. "Oh God, help me, I haven't had a
chance to find the secret of the jewels. I can't die yet," she
pleaded as they forced her to lie down on the old stone
altar.

She could see dried blood stains as she struggled to
get free, but she was overwhelmed and could struggle no
longer. They held her by the hands and legs, and the old
chief took up a long knife in his hands. In the seconds
that it took for the old man to pick up the knife, many
thoughts passed through Treaia's head. Why had this
man refused to accept the truth that had been told him at
the temple? Why did he believe he was right in what he
was doing now? As she lay there, bound by their hands,
she looked to the sky. There, circling high above, was a
bird. "Beautiful winged creature," she thought, "I wish I
could fly with you this moment, but soon my spirit will.
Oh mother, why did I want to change my life? How I wish I
were still at the temple! How I wish the gong would ring
now like before!"

The old man raised his knife to thrust into her heart,
but the chief was so old that his hand shook. He lowered
the knife, took a firmer grip, and once again started to
raise it, when suddenly there arose a large murmur in the
crowd. A thousand birds were descending on them,
screeching and pecking. Everyone began to run, includ-
ing the old chief, who had dropped the knife in disbelief.
Treaia jumped up from the altar and began running as
fast as she could, not knowing where she ran, just know-
ing that she must.

Treaia did not know how long or how far she ran, but

finally she had to sit down, with her heart pounding in her ears. After a while she looked around as she kept taking deep breaths, although it seemed she had no breath left. She realized she had run into a dark forest. "It doesn't matter," she said to herself. "Now I am safe. I'm so grateful to the wonderful creatures of Nature who rescued me, but now at last I must sleep." So Treaia gladly fell asleep, and she dreamed of her prince, not realizing what strange land she had run into.

Chapter Four

The Forest of Deception

Tartek rubbed his chin with one hand and tapped his fingers nervously with the other, gazing intently into his forest. "Yes, there she is," he said to himself, "sleeping in my kingdom. Perhaps now I will finally be able to get the jewels from her, and be free to come and go from here as I choose. But to get her to leave the jewels, how shall I begin?"

Now Tartek was no ordinary man, and he ruled no ordinary kingdom. His was a vast land, and he lived on the very edge of it in a huge castle made of hand-cut stone and crystal. You could not have told his age by looking at him, for all you would have seen would have been a blond handsomeness, unusual in its perfection. But in his light blue eyes was a coldness, an evilness, that was hard to believe. There was no kindness or love in those eyes, nor had there ever been.

Tartek did not remember the origin of his kingdom, nor did he care. In his kingdom he used a magic that trapped any wanderer, and this magic was his great secret and obsession. His magic lay in the power of illusion. He was able to create any terrible or beautiful apparition he wished, and to see through all material objects. The only thing he could not do was leave his own kingdom. So, for as long as he could remember—and he could not remember how long that was—he had been a prisoner in his own land.

Because of Tartek's power to see through material objects, he spent much of his time watching all the surrounding lands. He wanted to have power over these other lands also, for he was bored with just his own. Several times he tried to leave his kingdom and use his magic elsewhere, but each time he failed. One day, while he was watching events in a neighboring land, he had seen the jewels of the temple, and he knew that they contained the knowledge he did not possess. Tartek was cunning, and he realized that if he could acquire the jewels, the combination of his knowledge and the knowledge of the jewels would give him power not only over *his* land, but also over the others, and this was what he desired most.

He could not leave his kingdom, so he had sent his servants to invade the temple and bring back the jewels.

31

But they had failed because the jewels could not be stolen when they were in the possession and care of their keeper. When Tartek realized this, he gave up all hope of ever gaining possession of them, until one day he saw Treaia enter his forest. With his power to create illusion he was sure he could at last find a way to satisfy his desires. He rubbed his hands in glee.

"What an interesting dream, and so beautiful," Treaia thought, as she lay on the ground where she had fallen asleep. With her eyes still closed she went over what she could remember of the dream. "It seems that in the dream I had a twin," she said to herself, "but we were being raised apart. Every night we went together to a beautiful place. Somewhere a home was being prepared for us, and we were to be married. I can't remember, but I think his name began with an M sound."

Suddenly Treaia heard a rustling in the leaves, and she opened her eyes in fear. Fire was coming toward her—large, evil-looking, flickering tongues of flame. Of course, Treaia did not know she was in Tartek's forest, in the power of the master of illusion, and she jumped up and quickly ran farther into the forest to avoid the oncoming flames.

Then all of a sudden the fire was gone, and to her surprise Treaia found herself in the middle of a forest so thick and dense that she could not see the sun. It was getting very dark. "Oh, I wish I had someone to love me and take care of me. I'm so tired of being alone; I don't even know which way to go any more," thought Treaia. Then she began to hear strange discordant music, the most offensive sounds she had ever heard. As she listened, she noticed a darting, shooting greenish fire, which as she watched became eyes—green-fire eyes. Then she saw to her horror that the eyes were the eyes of skeletons. She could not seem to take her eyes off them as they danced in the air to the discordant music. They came closer and closer, and she could see their grotesque expressions and movements, which made her whole body shake with fear.

Suddenly she realized it was she they were after, so she turned and ran as fast as she could. "Ramana, what am I to do?" screamed Treaia, as she ran faster and faster. Every time she looked back the skeletons were getting closer. Now they were laughing at her with horrible wails, getting closer and closer still. Suddenly she came to a deep ravine and she had to stop short. She stood frozen, looking back at the horror and seeing sure death below. The terrifying dancers with the emerald-fire eyes kept advancing in their rhythmic pace. Treaia was so overwhelmed with fear that she fainted, but even in unconsciousness she held on tightly to the jewels.

Tartek watched her, proud of his horrifying illusion. And a new desire came upon him as he looked at the loveliness of Treaia. "I must have her *and* the jewels; I have never seen such beauty," Tartek said to the winds. "I will go and rescue her from the terror she has been through." Laughing, he called out for some of his servants.

Treaia lay very still, fearing to open her eyes. "What is that noise I hear?" she murmured. "It sounds like horses' hoofs beating on the ground." She opened her eyes and hesitantly tried to sit up. "Who is there? Who is coming?" she called out.

"A friend," Tartek replied. "I have come to help you." He brought his black stallion to a halt by Treaia. "Quickly mount behind me and I will take you to safety."

"Thank you, sir," Treaia said gratefully, as she climbed up behind him on the now prancing horse. The moment she was astride, the horse took off like the very wind itself. It was a fast, wild ride and Treaia clung tightly to Tartek's waist. When they reached the gates of the castle the horse slowed down and pawed the ground in impatience, while servants opened the gates wide for them to ride through. Other servants came running up and helped Treaia dismount. But to her surprise, Tartek rode off again into the distance.

"Where is my rescuer going?" Treaia asked the servants. "I wish to thank him."

"Don't worry, my dear, he has only gone to tend to the horse. He will return later," said the servant with a knowing look. "Come now, we will take you to your room where you can rest and refresh yourself."

Once inside the castle, Treaia realized she had never seen such grandeur. The servant led her up the huge, winding staircase, and Treaia was filled with wonder at all she saw. Finally they stopped at a beautifully carved door, which swung open, revealing a magnificent room—a room of splendor. There was a large bed in the center of the room, carved with roses and gilded. The carpet was pink, thick, and plush, and curtains of the thinnest fabric she had ever seen blew gently at the windows. There was a fireplace made from rose crystal that sparkled like diamonds. And each piece of furniture was covered with carved roses and gilded with gold.

"This is to be your room while you stay here," said the servant, noticing the pleased look on her face.

"It will be a pleasure, for it is the most beautiful room I have ever seen," exclaimed Treaia in awe.

Women servants came and helped her bathe. Food was brought for her, of the choicest fruits. The servants dressed her in a gown of silk, and put her to rest in the carved bed of roses, which had a mattress of the softest down. She slept the night without dreams, enjoying the luxury of the castle and the feeling of safety.

On waking the next morning she saw a woman servant standing at the foot of her bed. "Will my lady please be prepared to have breakfast with the master of the house?" asked the servant.

"Oh, gladly! I am anxious to thank him for saving me," Treaia said as she scurried out of bed to get ready. The servant dressed her in the loveliest blue gown, which seemed to float gracefully around her body, almost like a cloud. Her feet were fitted into dainty silk slippers. Another servant arrived to dress her hair in braids, with gold threads woven through. She felt like a beautiful lady as she was led down the stairs into the large dining room.

When she entered, she at first saw only the room. The walls were paneled with a rich, deep blue and gold; a large chandelier hung from the ceiling, dripping with dazzling crystals; and the furniture was made of fruitwood, with inlays of gold and silver. Then she saw him, as he rose to greet her from the far end of the table.

"How good it is of you to join me this morning," Tartek said in his most charming and polite fashion.

The night before it had been very dark when Treaia had climbed up on the horse, so this was really the first time that she had seen Tartek. "I have never seen such a handsome man," she thought to herself. And she said in nearly a whisper, "Kind sir, I am indeed grateful to you for saving me from the terror in the forest last night."

"It was my pleasure, my lady," said Tartek, bowing low. "Allow me to seat you by my side and we shall have breakfast." With that he gently took her arm and led her to a chair.

For a long time they ate in silence, glancing up once in a while to look at each other. Every time Treaia looked at Tartek he would smile at her, and his smile made him look so handsome that she never looked deep into his eyes.

Presently he said, "My lady, will you tell me your name and where you come from?"

"My name is Treaia, and I come from a temple a long way from here," she replied. She told him about the destruction of the temple and all her adventures since then. It had been so long since she had really talked to anyone that she poured out her heart to him. When she finally finished her story, she added, "And you, dear sir, please tell me of yourself."

"There is not much to tell," he replied. "My name is Tartek, and I am the lord of this land. It is usually very peaceful here except when some evil ones, who reside in the forest, cause trouble, and that is what happened last night. I am so very sorry that someone as lovely as you has had to bear such hardship, but at last you have come into a safe harbor." Tartek smiled his most handsome smile.

"Again, I am most grateful," Treaia said, feeling very pleased and secure.

"It is my wish that you should stay here for as long as you desire. The freedom of the castle and gardens is yours. My only request is that you should join me at meals, for I have been alone a long time and your company would give me much pleasure," implored Tartek.

Treaia was flattered to have such a man as Tartek admire her. Maybe all her dreams were coming true at last, she thought. Everything was so beautiful, and finally she felt she had found someone who wanted to take care of her. "If it pleases you, Tartek, I will stay, for I would like to repay you for your kindness," Treaia answered. Bowing low to conceal his smirk of delight, Tartek left the room, with a reminder to Treaia that they would meet again at dinner.

Treaia spent the day wandering from room to room and throughout the gardens. Each new thing she saw seemed to be more beautiful than the last. She was happy and safe. What a wonderful man Tartek was! Treaia was totally unaccustomed to the company of men, especially of handsome, charming men, and she felt lightheaded, almost giddy, and full of excitement. "What a wonderful way to live!" she thought.

Day after day Treaia enjoyed wandering around the castle, feeling totally carefree, and day after day she found new parts of the castle or gardens to explore. Each mealtime she spent in the blue and gold dining room with Tartek. They made pleasant conversation, and he always asked her what she had done since he had last seen her. Treaia began to wait anxiously for mealtimes, when she would be able to join him again.

One evening after they had eaten an exceptional meal, Tartek said, "Sweet Treaia, come and walk with me in the garden; I have something I must say to you."

Treaia joined him, and for a long time they strolled along the walkways, admiring the night-blooming flowers. It was very still in the garden.

"Tartek," Treaia said in a hushed voice, "it has puzzled me that I never see any birds in the garden. Can you tell me why?"

He looked surprised for a moment but was quick to answer her. "My dear, I use magic to keep anything from spoiling the beauty of the garden for you," he laughed, saying this as if it were a joke. When he told her how he cared for her, even in a joking manner, she blushed and promptly forgot about the birds. She only laughed and said, "You are a dear man to try to please me like that."

"I would like to please you always," Tartek said seriously. "If you will have me, I would like you to become my wife, for I have grown to love you. Everything in the kingdom will be yours."

"Oh Tartek, I believe I am growing to love you also.

But I have nothing to give you in return except what I am beginning to feel," Treaia replied earnestly.

"I want you only as you came to me, my love," he said, and he leaned over and kissed her tenderly on the lips. He led her back into the castle, and called all the servants to him. "Prepare for a grand wedding," he ordered them. "Treaia is to be my wife and your new mistress. One week from today the wedding feast will begin." Then he dismissed the servants and saw Treaia back to her room. As they said goodnight, Tartek was secretly delighted that his plan to gain his twin desires was about to succeed.

But Treaia lay restless in her bed that night. Her thoughts were confused. "Was I wrong to accept Tartek's proposal?" she asked herself. "I feel as though I am beginning to love him. He is good to me, and he loves and cares for me. He has offered me his kingdom for nothing in return, so why do I feel so restless? This is surely just what I want. I should feel happy with the idea of being his wife. It's true that when he kissed me, I felt very little, but that will grow in time, I'm sure."

Treaia went to sleep this way and her dreams were troubled. Sometimes in her dreams she was with Ramana when Ramana had given her the jewels. Then she had a dream of a wedding in a triangle-shaped building, in which she was the bride and the prince with the sword was the groom. It was a beautiful wedding and she and the groom seemed to blend together, almost as if they were one. She awoke and lay in her bed thinking of the dream. "Marriage is supposed to make two as one," she said to herself. "Why do I dream of someone I do not know? I feel so confused tonight."

Over on the other side of the castle sat Tartek, feeling very pleased with himself. His plan of pursuit had worked well. He leaned back and started to relax, thinking that both the jewels and Treaia would soon be his, but an unexpected element was creeping into the plan. He knew that he desired Treaia, but this new feeling puzzled him. He had grown to care for her.

The servants were busy organizing the wedding, which was to be held in a few days, and Treaia spent many hours being fitted for her wedding clothes. As usual, she spent mealtimes with Tartek, and they walked in the garden more frequently now that they were to be wed. She enjoyed being with him, and he seemed more relaxed and happy than she had ever seen him. She tried to forget about her silly worries of that night.

It was the day before the wedding and Treaia was restless again. She couldn't seem to sit still. So, the feeling arose in her that she should go exploring around the castle, which she had always enjoyed. She went through room after room, searching for what she did not know, but driven onward by an invisible force. Sometimes the beauty of everything she saw made her wonder. "How can everything be so very perfect?" she said to herself. She had been taught that nothing was ever completely perfect on this planet, but that did not seem to be true in Tartek's kingdom. "Maybe Ramana was wrong," she thought.

Then suddenly she came across a small door. She knew it was a door because she saw light coming from beneath it; otherwise she would have walked right past it. She pushed and the door opened. Inside she was taken completely by surprise, for everything in the room was covered with cobwebs. As she looked around in amazement, she saw many art objects, statues, and paintings, all scattered about in great disorder and confusion. "Very strange," thought Treaia, as she looked about her. "Why is this room so unlike the others? But what's that? I know that statue! It looks like one that we used to have at the temple." She went closer, hardly believing her eyes. "The statue looks the same, but of course it can't be. The one at the temple was stolen." Her heart began to beat faster. "Yes, the one at the temple was stolen. What could that mean?" She began to examine everything in the room. "Oh God," she cried out, "there's another one! That painting used to hang by the altar! How could it be? How could it be? I must talk to Tartek about this," she decided, leaving the room hurriedly.

She quickly found a servant and asked him, "Have you seen your master? I need to speak to him very urgently."

"No, mistress, I do not know where he is. I only know

that he will return for the evening meal as usual," said the servant, as he bowed and left.

Treaia spent the rest of the afternoon in her room, thinking of what she had found. "How could our things from the temple have reached this land?" she asked herself. "What did Ramana say about an evil man? But Tartek could not be that man—he is so good to me. But what if he is, then what should I do?" She paced the floor until it was time to join Tartek for dinner. She decided to say nothing for a while.

As she entered the dining room Tartek came to greet her with a smile on his face. Then he noticed her strange expression. "Come, my dear," he said, "whatever could make you look so troubled?" He put his arm around her shoulders, and led her to the table. Treaia was so silent during the meal that Tartek took her out into the garden for a walk to find out what was bothering her. As they were walking, he thought, "I have not been checking on Treaia lately, as I did when she first came. But why should I? She is happy here and wants to marry me. My plan succeeded perfectly." He picked a flower and handed it to Treaia. "Please, my dear, what has been bothering you today?" he said sweetly. "Tomorrow we are to be wed and nothing must spoil the occasion."

At first Treaia did not know what to say. Then she realized that something did bother her, something she had not thought of openly. "Tartek, why is it that we are to be married and yet I see you only at meals? In fact that is the only time that I have ever seen you," she said, and she looked straight and deep into his eyes. She was shocked at the evil she saw there, but tried to hide her consternation out of fear.

"What can I tell her?" Tartek wondered. "I cannot tell her the truth, which is that, in order to keep up the perfection of the beauty I have created for her, I must spend many hours a day in deep concentration. Since the evening she consented to marry me, I have relaxed my concentration and spent more time with her. After we are married, I will find a way to leave this kingdom, for then I will have the knowledge of the jewels to help me. I will take her to another land where I will be able to spend my time, all my time, with her, and we will live together in real splendor." But to Treaia he lied and said, "My dear, it takes a lot of time to run a land as big as my kingdom, but once we are wed things will change. We will travel and see all the world."

Treaia let him think that this satisfied her. "I see. I'm so sorry, I should not have interfered in your work. Now please excuse me. I must get some rest so that I will be beautiful for our wedding tomorrow," she said with a smile on her face.

Once in her room she broke down and sobbed, "Oh Ramana, I almost married the man who caused your death. When I looked into his eyes I never saw anything so evil. Why did I notice nothing before?" She still held in her hand the flower that Tartek had given her, and she lifted it to her nose to smell it, out of habit, but it had no smell. "This flower is not real!" she cried, and as she looked at it, it crumbled to nothing in her hand. " 'Face illusion,' Ramana told me, 'and it will disappear,' " she remembered. "But what causes illusion? Desire. Yes, I desired to have someone care for me and love me. I wanted a different and exciting life. Tartek seemed so kind and handsome. Why didn't I notice what was behind those eyes? Because of his flattery, that's why. He flattered my vanity; he made my desire for a different way of life cloud everything else. 'Desire distorts or hides truth,' Ramana told me. Ramana! Forgive me for being deceived. My selfish desire for excitement and someone to care for me has caused me to be blinded by Tartek and his illusions. My desire started at home and led me here. Why didn't I remember your words, 'Desire causes misery, all misery. Aspire to be, do not desire to have. Without aspiration there is no growth.' "

Suddenly her thoughts of Ramana were gone and Treaia returned to the present. "I must get out of here, but how?" she thought. "I can go out of the front door of the castle, since it will be quite a while before dark. If I see anyone, I'll say I couldn't rest because I am excited about the wedding. I'll wear the tunic I came in; the other clothes might be nothing but dust after I leave this land." She crept silently down the stairs, out of the front door, and headed into the forest. "What if I meet with the terror I saw before?" she suddenly remembered. But in the next instant she realized that Tartek must have caused that too. Everything was clear to her at last. Once in the forest, she ran as fast as she could through the trees.

Meanwhile Tartek sat in his room thinking with delight of the wedding, the jewels, and his conquest of Treaia, and he decided to look in on her to see if she was resting properly. In concentration, he looked through the walls of the castle and into her room. She was not there! In a panic he searched through all the rooms in the castle, and then through the gardens. The more he looked, the more upset he became. Finally he began to search the forest. There she was, wearing the tunic she had come in, running as fast as she could. This meant only one thing to Tartek: she must know of his deception. With all the speed that he had, he ran to the stable and mounted his black stallion. Without stopping for saddle or bridle, he jumped up and raced like the wind to follow Treaia, determined not to let her escape him.

As Treaia ran on, she suddenly heard horses' hoofs pounding behind her. "No, it can't be!" she thought in despair. "Tartek didn't see me leave. It cannot be he." She ran faster and faster, but the sounds came closer and closer, until suddenly she felt herself being lifted into the air by a pair of strong arms that held her fast. Exhausted, she could do nothing but sob as Tartek carried her back to the castle in triumph.

When they reached the castle courtyard, Tartek jumped down from his horse, holding on to Treaia tightly. Panting and out of breath, he dragged her into the castle and pushed her into a sitting room. "Why do you wish to leave me, my dear?" he asked, gazing down at her with a strange look on his face.

Slowly Treaia began to speak. "To think that I thought I was beginning to love you—you who caused Ramana and the others to be murdered. Ramana told me to face illusion and illusion will disappear, but the evil in you will never disappear, because it is no illusion, it is real," she said bravely. She looked at a bouquet of flowers on one of the tables. They withered instantly and were gone. "See, they were not real!" she cried. "Nothing is real here in your land."

"You are right," said Tartek in a low, menacing

voice. "Nothing here is real, but the lands I will conquer when you give me the jewels will be real. You are upset now, but when you have time to think you will see that marrying me is the only way out for you. I will have you *and* the jewels. But if you want reality, I shall take you somewhere very real."

He grabbed her arm and led her through room after room, until they came to a flight of stairs leading down into darkness. Lighting a candle, he pulled her behind him down the winding steps. All was darkness except for the flickering of the candle. Down, down they went, until it seemed to Treaia that they could go no farther. Finally, she realized they were walking on flat ground again, and winding in and out of passages. They were in a gigantic labyrinth! As they walked, Tartek stopped and looked into the caverns, as if he were searching for something.

"I was right," he said finally, pushing Treaia into a cavelike room. "This room has running water. To keep alive, my pet, you shall need water. Ah, look up there, you shall even have light. The sun sends a beam through the hole in the ceiling." He looked at Treaia almost lovingly, "Will you come back and marry me now, or will you stay down here, where all will soon be dark?"

"I will never come to you, I would rather die first," Treaia said scornfully.

"Have it your own way then," said Tartek. "When you are tired and hungry, pick up a rock, pound on that wall, and I will hear its echo and come for you. If you try to leave this room you will get lost in the dark caverns and be without water, and I will be waiting for you." With that, he turned and left her alone.

Treaia stood still and listened to Tartek's footsteps grow fainter, until she heard no sound but the drip of water. Very little light came in through the shaft at the top. Cautiously she took a step or two and felt that the floor was quite smooth to her feet. To keep herself busy, she began to explore the room. She found that the walls were rough in some spots and smooth in others, and that they were damp from the moisture that she guessed came from the water running down one wall. She went over to the strange stone container that caught the water and put her finger in it cautiously; it felt cool to her touch. Cupping her hands, she scooped up some water and tasted it, and to her surprise, it tasted sweet and fresh. Looking around the room, she saw that one corner was completely dark; no light at all shone on it. She moved herself over to the darkness and began inching herself into it, until at last she felt a wall. "Nothing here," she thought. But on her legs she began to feel cool air, so she dropped to her hands and knees and felt around. "Yes, here is an opening in the wall," she said to herself. "If there is cool air, maybe this is a way out."

Then suddenly she heard the sound of hissing. She listened and could tell that the opening was full of snakes, so she quickly made her way back out to the center of the room where there was some light, realizing that it would soon be pitch black.

"What can I do?" she asked herself in despair. "What choice do I have?" Tears started rolling down her face. The events of the day came over her and she began to shake and cry. The more she shook the more she cried. At last there were no tears left, and she had to face up to the position she was in. "Ramana, what can I do?" she said to the bare dark walls. "I can't marry Tartek, knowing he caused you to die. I could just sit here until I die of starvation. Then there's the opening, but it's full of snakes, although they must be able to get out somehow. Maybe they aren't real and only one of Tartek's illusions. But if they are real, I'll surely die if I go in there. I've failed you, Ramana. I even gave up the idea of finding the secret of the jewels to marry Tartek. But I know I'd rather die of the snakes than stay where Tartek is."

Somehow it had helped her to talk to Ramana. It was dark now, and all she could see was the soft light she emitted from within herself. Ramana had shown her how all living things emit their own light. "Why didn't I remember that? Then I would have seen through the illusion much faster. But just sitting here thinking like this is not going to help me one way or the other," thought Treaia. She took a deep breath, and her light became brighter. Then she remembered that Ramana had shown her how to increase her light with breaths taken in a certain way. Treaia took another deep breath and made her way over to the opening where the snakes were. Hesitantly she peered into the passage.

"Yes, the snakes are real," she thought. "I can see light glowing from them. But, if I can attune myself with them, they will know I mean them no harm." She sat very still for a moment or two, then took a deep breath and proceeded into the passage. Oh, the passage was thick with them; they were intertwined with one another. Treaia took another deep breath, trying to emit enough light to see where she was crawling. The opening was not large enough for her to stand up, so she inched herself along, feeling the snakes slither over her arms and legs. "These are God's creatures too, as I am," she told herself. "Oh snakes, I shall try not to hurt you, but you are so many in this small passage." She kept going, thinking of nothing but attunement with the snakes, and taking very deep breaths. She seemed to spend forever crawling among the snakes. She had to go so slowly, so slowly.

Suddenly she saw a light, moonlight—she had almost made it. "No, don't think of anything but attunement until you are out," she kept telling herself. Another deep breath and she moved on. At last she was outside in the fresh air, with the stars above her. Free from the danger of the snakes, she started shaking violently, and perspiration broke out on her forehead. "Thank you, God, I never thought I could do it," she whispered. "Now if I could only find my way out of this land of Tartek's before he finds I am gone." She turned and ran.

The last time Tartek had looked in on Treaia with his special vision, she had still been sitting in the middle of the room. Later he decided to check on her again. "She's gone!" he cried in disbelief, searching throughout the caverns. Unable to find her, he aimed his gaze back into the room, then into the passage that hid the snakes. "No, she couldn't have gone through the snakes; no one could," he thought. "That was the reason I chose that room." Not finding her anywhere else, he looked past the snakes in the passage and out the other side. There she was, running as fast as her long, agile legs could carry her. Although Treaia knew it not, she was already across the boundaries of Tartek's kingdom, and he could no longer reach her. He became livid with rage, sweeping the objects on his desk to the floor, and pounding the wall with his fists. "I'll find a way to get you, Treaia," he yelled. "No one else shall ever have you, or the jewels."

Chapter Five

Less Real

Treaia ran in a frenzy the rest of that night, getting as far away from the evil kingdom as possible. She did not know how far the Forest of Deception stretched, or even if she would ever come to the end of it. The farther she ran, the more feverish and delirious she became, seeing Tartek in every shadow. When dawn came, she was still moving, although much more slowly now. Suddenly she saw in the new day's light a lake with the morning sun sparkling on its blue-green smoothness, and she realized how thirsty she was. Her body ached from running and felt as though it was burning with fire from the fever that was taking over. She made her way toward the lake as quickly as she could, stumbling and falling several times before she reached the water's edge. She reached over and splashed the cool, refreshing water on her face and hands, but she could no longer contend with the terrors of the night. Her body began to feel as though it didn't belong to her any more, and she fainted into uncertain darkness.

Feeling movement about her, Treaia opened her eyes very slowly, fearing Tartek may be standing over her. "Oh," she gasped in surprise, because there in front of her stood several children, perhaps a dozen, staring at her with an intense look in their startling eyes. The children had large, round black eyes and blond hair, almost white. Their hair was very long, which made them look less naked. Quickly remembering her manners, Treaia said, "Hello, my name is Treaia," hoping to learn who these curious children were.

They did not speak to her, but began to draw closer to her and touch her hair and face, smiling at her as they did so. Then they pulled Treaia to her feet and danced about, holding hands with her and each other. Standing among these strange yet pleasingly pretty children, who were having such a good time, Treaia felt relaxed and confident again. The children soon grew tired of jumping about and began to push and tug at her, leading her into the lake. "Yes, it will feel so good to be clean again—a bath is a very good idea," thought Treaia.

"Please, children, don't pull so hard," laughed Treaia, but her laughter soon died away. "Children, please stop! Don't pull me under," she pleaded in fear. The children did not reply but pulled her farther and farther and deeper and deeper into the water. Treaia began to struggle even harder, as it became more difficult to keep her head above water. Finally she took one last gasp of air and became completely submerged in the water. The children still held on to her, pulling her down, down, down, until they reached the bottom of the lake. "If I don't take a breath, my lungs will burst; and if I do I will surely drown," thought Treaia. But she could not hold her breath any longer and was forced to take a breath; to her astonishment she found she was breathing perfectly normally.

"We could not speak to you before, but now that we are back in our own world we are able to. My name is Helena and this is Boreno," the girl said, pointing to the boy beside her. Then she began bouncing from one child to the next, telling Treaia each one's name.

"Where are you taking me?" Treaia asked, forgetting for the moment the miracle that she could breathe under water, and getting caught up once again in the children's excitement.

"We are taking you to see our mother. Where else would we take you?" said Boreno, looking almost annoyed at Treaia for asking.

"Why does your mother want to see me?" Treaia asked, hoping this question would not also annoy the boy.

"She wants to know about the Great Ones. I have never seen the Great Ones, I have only heard our mother speak of them, so don't ask any more silly questions," said Boreno.

They moved easily through the water, in a strange strolling fashion. "What exotic plants," thought Treaia, as she began to notice the delicate, lacy, floating ferns, and the different colored flowers opening and closing gracefully in the movement of the water. Little schools of fish, all shimmery and shiny, were flitting in and out among them. Light streamed down in rays of moving golden luminescence.

"Not much farther," said Helena, as she gently pulled on Treaia to hurry. Just then they rounded another patch of waving plants, and she added, "There is our home."

"Oh, how very beautiful," Treaia said, as she sucked in her breath in amazement. There stood a castle with tall towers and turrets. The castle looked as though it was made of glass, or were they simply bubbles that she saw, looking like round transparent stones? It was hard to tell. And colors streamed out from the castle as if from many prisms, reflecting everywhere she looked, until it felt as though she was walking through a world of moving color and light.

As they approached the castle, the children began giggling and twittering and pulling her faster in their hurry to get to their mother. Toward them walked a tall woman in a filmy, shimmering green covering that flowed around her; she had the same long white hair and large round black eyes, although if black could be blacker, hers were.

"At last, my children, you have finally brought her," the lady said, as she reached down and affectionately patted the children who had run up to her. "Quickly now, Helena, as you are the oldest you may introduce me to our guest."

"This is Treaia; Treaia this is our mother, the Lake Mother," said Helena, extending her arm in a welcoming fashion.

"How do you do," said Treaia, wondering how Helena could be the oldest when they all seemed to be the same size, and looked almost alike.

"Please sit down, my dear, I have been waiting for you," said the Lake Mother in a musical voice, as she herself sat on what looked like a large bubble.

Treaia looked behind her and saw another bubble chair and sat down as she was asked. The children were jumping and tumbling about with one another until the Lake Mother clapped her hands, when the children very quickly found themselves a spot to sit in front of their mother and Treaia.

Looking intently at Treaia, the Lake Mother asked, "Have you ever been to the sea?" her large eyes almost swallowing Treaia in the desire to know.

"Well, yes," stammered Treaia, startled, "I used to live by the sea."

The Lake Mother sighed a deep sigh of relief. "I have been wishing for someone to come who knows of the sea," she said. "That is why my children brought you to me, in the hope that you had knowledge of that large body of water where the Great Ones live."

"What Great Ones, Mother?" Treaia asked, puzzled.

"What Great Ones?" said the Lake Mother in surprise. "Why, the dolphins and their larger friends, of course."

"I have seen them, but only at a distance, and only on two or three occasions when I was a small child, but I enjoy just remembering the smiling playful creatures," answered Treaia. "I wonder why she calls the dolphins and whales the Great Ones," she thought to herself, not wishing to ask too many questions.

"Please tell me more of what they look like and what they do," enquired the Mother.

"Well, they are fish-shaped and longer than myself, but they breathe air," said Treaia. "Not many creatures who live in the sea breathe air. Their skin is smooth and shiny silver-gray. They love to jump high and play with each other, and they make high-pitched squeaking sounds. As for the whales, I've only seen them from a great distance. They have spouts that spray water high into the air. Whales also breathe air, but they stay underwater a long time. They are so large that they would not be able to live in this lake." But as she said this, she began to wonder, "How is it that these people are here, and why can I breathe underwater?"

But before Treaia could ask these questions, the Lake Mother began to speak. "That is very interesting. I asked them what they looked like and all I could understand was that they were quite large compared with the other creatures they lived with. It doesn't seem to matter what our form is or where we exist. Our awareness is the important thing," she mused, almost to herself.

The Lake Mother suddenly seemed to have a burst of inspiration and asked, "Could you draw pictures of them for me here in the sand?" handing Treaia a pointed rock to draw with. Treaia used the rock and to the best of her ability drew the dolphins and whales she had seen.

"How is it you can talk to the dolphins, and where did you hear about them?" she asked curiously.

"Oh, from them," the Lake Mother answered, but seeing the look on Treaia's face smiled and went on, "through attunement, and learning to understand what I was attuned to. You know about attunement; words, sounds, thoughts are all vibrations, so my consciousness just attuned to more subtle states of thought; I picked up their wavelengths a long time ago and ever since I have been trying to know them better. It really is very interesting that dolphins look like fish, but then who's to say what even higher states of consciousness might look like?"

Treaia then started thinking of what she had learned about attunement, and what fun it would be to try if she ever got to see a dolphin or whale again. Then one of the children pulled Treaia off her bubble chair. "Come, it's our turn now, let's go and visit the Guardian of the Cave," Helena said, and she and all the children started dancing and shouting. There wasn't even time for Treaia to say goodbye to their mother, although she tried to wave as the children laughingly dragged her off.

They had not gone far when they turned a corner of swaying bushes, and darkness seemed to engulf them. The children were murmuring and giggling to each other. One of them took her hand, for which she was very grateful. "Don't be scared, we will be in the cavern soon, and then it will be light again," whispered one of the children, as they gently pulled her along a dark path. A purple haze began to be visible, and as they walked it became brighter and brighter until they were inside a gigantic cavern covered with amethyst crystals hanging side by side as close as they could be. The brilliant stones covering the ceiling and walls grew like grass, but instead of green, they ranged from the very lightest lavender to the deepest purple. A woman sat before a small fire in the center of the cavern. The flames of the fire darted from one amethyst crystal to another until the large room was filled with a scintillating purple, like purple circles constantly on the move.

The children led Treaia to the woman. "This is the Guardian of the Cave of Circles," said Helena as she nudged Treaia forward. "And this is Treaia, whom we brought to see our mother so she could tell her about the Great Ones."

"I believe I learned more about the Great Ones than anyone," thought Treaia fleetingly, bowing to the woman. Treaia felt slightly dizzy as she watched the purple circles flashing around the cavern. It was hard to make out what the woman looked like, since the purple never held still quite long enough; but her voice was smooth and rich and very clear, as she said, "I am so glad to meet you, and it is good to see you children again. Sit down and let us begin the visit."

"Sit down, sit down," chanted the children, as they helped Treaia to the floor of the cave, and all crowded around her, looking up expectantly at the Guardian of the Cave.

"Ask me a riddle," called out one of the children.

"What is it that travels endlessly and is always the same distance from its home?" questioned the Guardian, smiling.

"Oh, that one is easy. You asked it before," Boreno said.

"I know, it's a circle," giggled another child.

"Let me ask something; it's my turn," Helena said as she jumped up and down.

"Please do," said the Guardian.

"What is the largest kingdom on our planet?" Helena asked, and sat back with folded arms, very pleased with herself.

No one spoke for quite a few minutes as everyone tried to think. "No one answered. I get to answer. It's water," squealed Helena in delight.

"I remember now," said Boreno, sullenly. "You learned that from our mother."

"Do you have a question, or perhaps you could share something with us during our visit," the Guardian said, leaning over close to Treaia's face.

Now that Treaia could see her face, she noticed that it was almost like stone, smooth and firm looking, but her eyes seemed to be like the jewels that hung from the ceiling, changing purple and shooting out rays of light.

"What is a rainbow?" Treaia asked and sat back to await the answer.

"Why, a rainbow is an arc that shows bands of color," answered one of the children, clapping hands.

"Wrong, it's a bridge," Treaia said, and looked all around at the strange looks on the children's faces. "Why did I say that? I feel so strange; it must be the purple circles. I wonder if I said something wrong?" thought Treaia.

"It's my turn now. What is truth? What is real?" asked the Guardian, and as she spoke her eyes seemed to grow to twice their size.

"What is truth? What is real? All is truth, all is real," answered Treaia.

"How can all be truth, or all be real?" laughed the Guardian.

"If everything is, it is, and that is the truth and is real," Treaia said, still not knowing quite what she was saying or why, but words just kept coming out of her mouth.

"You say a rainbow is a bridge. I say it is an arc or a circle of color. Would you like to see for yourself?" said the Guardian.

Before Treaia could accept or decline, the Guardian made a motion with her hand and Treaia found herself in a bubble floating up to the ceiling. Looking down, she could see the children jumping up and down and enjoying the whole thing. She marveled as she floated up through the ceiling and then through the water, and up and up into the sky, higher and higher. And there was a rainbow, a beautiful arc of colors made by the sun shining through the moisture of the clouds. Now she was high above the clouds and she looked down; to her astonishment she could see the entire rainbow, and she realized that it was a full circle. "Is that what the Guardian was trying to tell me," she asked herself, "that I must always rise above something to understand it? If the rainbow was a bridge, and if I had walked upon it, and if I had kept walking, I would have come back to myself."

Treaia mused to herself, enjoying the wonderful free feeling of flight above the clouds, when she realized that for no apparent reason she was no longer in her bubble and she was falling very fast. "Help, help me someone!" she called out in terror.

Then she sat straight up with a start, her heart still pounding rapidly, "What a strange dream!"

Chapter Six

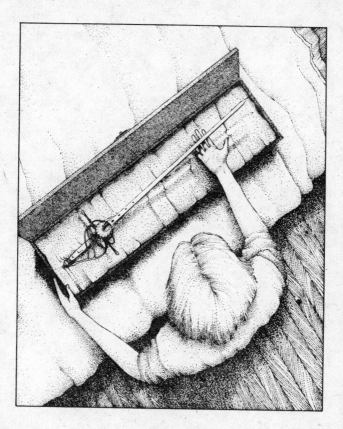

Mey

Meanwhile, on the same day that Ramana had found Treaia in the temple garden, far away a king was walking in his garden, as he usually did in the early evening. The garden was at its loveliest at this time of day, when the setting sun cast a pinkish-gold on the clouds overhead. King Almar's land was large, with the ocean to the west and steep cliffs to the south, and in between lay a spacious valley, with trees gently waving in the breezes. It was a tranquil landscape.

The king was a man of middle stature, who appeared taller because he always held himself in an upright, straight fashion. He was a man of middle years, with gray tipping the sides of his brow. King Almar was satisfied with his life, except for the sorrow of losing his wife and son in childbirth. All of King Almar's kingdom was satisfied; the people were content for the most part with the way things were. They were a people who never questioned. Why should they? There was always plenty of what they needed. Food grew in abundance; the countryside teemed with wildlife for the hunters; and everyone enjoyed eating, hunting, and once in a while a game or two. Aside from this they lived a very languid existence. In their satisfied state they were not aware of this, because the kingdom had been this way for a very long time, at least since before King Almar's father's father.

As King Almar walked this evening, he was thinking of a dream he had had the night before, in which he had been told that he was to have a son and that he would name him Mey. "Mey, what a strange name," he thought. "I must have been dreaming because of my sorrow over my wife. I need an heir or there will be no one to become king after I die, which would cause great problems for my people. But I don't want to marry again either; no one can take my beloved wife's place. Ah, how I wish I had a son."

As the king was thinking these thoughts he began to smell a perfume in the air—so delicate, so sweet. As he was sniffing the air, he began to discern sweet strains of music. He looked toward the wooded area by the garden where the sounds seemed to be coming from, and he suddenly saw a golden whirlwind rise out of the trees. Never having seen anything like this before, he hurried over and scanned the tops of the trees, but found nothing—the whirlwind was gone. Then he heard a sound down on the ground by his feet. As he looked, there—holding up its small arms and smiling at him—was a boy child.

King Almar picked up the child and marveled at the beauty he held in his arms—dark shining hair, olive complexion, and the most beautiful dark eyes the king had ever seen. As the king looked into these eyes, he said, "You are the dream I had. You shall be called Mey and declared Prince Mey before all the land."

In the land of King Almar, events, even mysterious events, were accepted easily. Finding the boy made the king so happy that he never questioned where the child had come from.

All the people of the land were called for the celebration and ceremony to crown the boy Prince Mey. Of course they never questioned, for King Almar was held to be the wisest man in the land. The people enjoyed themselves in many ways, some in sports on the grassy turf, some in games of skill, others in dancing and singing. Everyone rejoiced throughout the land. The king had the best time of all, for he was playing with the child, Mey.

Being a busy man, the king could not spend much of his time with Mey, so he put Mey in the charge of many servants. Everyone at the palace was so grateful there was an heir that the young prince's every whim was indulged. They didn't question if it was good for a young boy always to have his way. The young prince grew into a handsome, healthy, strong lad, since the very best of the land was always available to him. Not much was asked of Mey, because he was a prince, and everything was always done for him. In spite of being spoiled, Mey was not a mean boy. However, he was very mischievous, adventuresome, and sometimes overbearing with the people around him.

One day when Mey was about seven years old, he was sitting in the garden thinking about a small green creature a boy had shown him the day before. It was called a frog. "I must have a frog, maybe two," he said to himself. "If I can escape the servants and capture a frog, then all the boys will think I am very important." When the servants were busy talking, off he went as quickly as his seven-year-old legs would carry him in the direction of the pond. What a wondrous feeling of triumph came over his heart when he caught his first frog. Quickly he went on and caught more and more. He was proud indeed. So he continued all afternoon, capturing one frog after another, until there were almost forty. Satisfied at last, he headed home. How proud he felt!

All the servants were out searching for him, so he was able to sneak into his rooms without being caught. He quickly transferred his catch into a bag and washed himself, just enough to look presentable for dinner. As he was whistling and walking down the stairs to the dining room he met his father coming up.

"Where have you been, my son?" asked the king, putting his arms around Mey in relief.

"Nowhere special, father," Mey said, but inside he knew he had been somewhere special. The feeling of conquest filled his whole chest.

King Almar turned around and led Mey to the dining room. Mey, though usually talkative, was very silent as he ate his meal, a smile coming to his lips now and then. All of a sudden, dozens of yells and shrieks were let loose outside the dining room. The king and Mey ran out to see what had happened. There in the hall and on the staircase were Mey's frogs, all forty of them, jumping and leaping about.

Almar did not become angry with his son. How could he, when he saw the proud look on Mey's face as he leaped around with the frogs. But by the next morning Mey had learned how fast news travels. Every boy in the city knew that Mey had caught more frogs than any boy in the history of the kingdom. No one knew exactly how many, some said a hundred, others said a thousand. But it didn't really matter how many. Mey was known thereafter as the champion frog catcher.

How proud Mey felt at his success and his new reputation! Not only was he the prince and beloved by all, but he began to feel that he was cleverer than all the other boys in the kingdom, that he alone could conquer any obstacle he wished. Although his friends and his servants loved him dearly, it saddened them to see Mey become boastful and arrogant, since some of them suspected that Mey still had much to learn, and they saw that his self-importance could only make things more difficult for him.

Mey was about twelve when he traveled with his father and a large group of servants to the southern part of their kingdom. Mey and his friends were allowed to ride their horses and explore the surrounding areas from their campsite. Since Mey loved riding, they went off every day.

Finally they reached the border of the kingdom, a huge mountainous area with steep cliffs. Mey was immediately drawn to the lure of those heights.

"Let's begin the climb," Mey said with enthusiasm.

"Don't be foolish, no one can climb that mountain," said one of the boys.

"My father said it's been tried and there isn't any way," said another.

"You're all just scared! I'll bet I can do it," Mey said, swaggering with self-importance. "When I reach the top and wave down to you, you'll all feel very sorry you didn't come."

Mey took a rope and began to climb, but after just a little way he was already sorry he had been so boastful. "I must do it now, at all costs," he thought, finding a fingerhold here and there and heaving his young body up a tiny step farther. This went on all day, as Mey crept slowly and painfully up the face of the cliff. Finally he threw his rope over a rock and tried to pull himself up, but his strength gave out and he could not. He was stuck on a tiny ledge, holding onto the rope, trying to keep his balance with his legs.

"What can I do now?" he thought. "Nothing. If I let go, I'll be killed. I can't go any farther, and I can't go down either. What a fool I've made of myself!"

"Help! Help down there," Mey called in a frantic plea. "I don't know how long I can hang on."

At the base of the cliff the other youngsters, who had been waiting and watching, heard Mey in trouble, and some of them rode off for help.

It was getting dark when King Almar and some of his men finally rode up.

"Please hurry," cried Mey, in fear for his life.

King Almar picked four of his strongest men to climb after Mey. Up the face of the cliff, two or three feet at a time, they pulled themselves, and laboriously made their way over to Mey. Mey hung onto the rope and the crumbling ledge. He had stopped shouting and waited silently and shamefacedly for the men to reach him. Then two firm hands grasped his waist, and the men lowered Mey carefully down the cliff.

The king was not angry, just grateful that his son was alive and well. "After all, boys will be boys," he thought. But Mey rode back to camp in silence, knowing in his heart that he had failed and made a fool of himself in front of everyone.

As Mey grew expert in his riding technique, King Almar began taking him on some of his hunting expeditions. Hunting was one of the things the king enjoyed most; another was his accuracy with the bow. Almar had tried to interest Mey in hunting and to teach him bowmanship, as his own father had taught him. He told Mey how to focus or aim his thought at a target, and how to try to maintain his concentration in spite of distractions. But Mey found no interest in hunting, and the bow seemed too difficult and trying and he soon gave up any real effort to learn. This disappointed the king, but he hoped that in time Mey would learn to enjoy hunting and develop a fondness for the bow.

Next to riding his horse, the thing Mey enjoyed most of all was asking questions. "Father, why is the sky blue? Father, why is the grass green?" He had asked questions ever since he had learned to talk. The king would answer simply, "Because it is," or "Because it has always been." But his answers never satisfied Mey. He asked everyone questions, but he always got the same answer. The servants sometimes hid around corners when they saw Mey coming, so as not to be besieged by his questions.

One evening as they sat at dinner, Mey asked a new question. "Father, while I was exploring in the older tower today I found an old parchment," he said. "On this parchment was written DO NOT BE SELF-CENTERED. BE CENTERED IN SELF. Can you tell me what that means?"

Now the king knew how Mey liked to ask questions

about everything, but this question somehow seemed different. "What *does* it mean?" Almar wondered. "Who could have written it? Why does Mey always ask so many questions? I and the other people in the kingdom do not. Why don't we?" The king at last began to ask questions himself.

"My son, ever since you were able to talk you have questioned everything. Because of this last question, I myself have begun to wonder about some things. Will you please tell me why you question everything?" King Almar said with a puzzled look on his face.

"Father, ever since I can remember I have had dreams, dreams that are mysterious to me, that I do not quite understand. But I try to find out about things. It seems to me very important to understand and know all that is," answered Mey.

"I do not know the answers to your questions," said Almar excitedly, "but if we start looking together, perhaps we will find answers."

"Thank you, father, there is nothing I would rather share with you than learning," smiled Mey.

King Almar's search for answers began slowly. At first he spent an hour or so each day with Mey; they asked each other about things they didn't know and looked through whatever books were close at hand. Then one day Almar remembered that there was a large library in his castle, which had been closed up and unused for hundreds of years. He had the servants reopen the library, and clean and dust it. "Why was it ever closed?" Almar asked himself. "Perhaps because of contentment. When people are contented, they lose interest in searching for anything." The more King Almar learned, the more he found there was to learn. He searched through old records and tried to decipher them. Once the thirst for learning began, he could not quench it.

"To think that I had to become an old man before I discovered that learning could bring me such pleasure," the king said to Mey, putting his arm around his son in affection. "Come, let us go to the library. I would like to show you a most interesting book I have discovered."

So the years passed and Mey grew into a young man. One day King Almar and Prince Mey were riding in the hills above the palace. The king said, "I have ridden over this land many times in my life, but today it is more magnificent than I have ever seen it. I believe that my new understanding of things is the reason for this. When we understand something that is beautiful, it becomes even more beautiful. Son, I have much in this life to be thankful for, but you are the greatest blessing ever bestowed on me. For without you I would have gone all my life and never questioned; I would never have even begun to learn about the world we live in. Thank you."

But Mey cried out in alarm, "Father, look toward the palace! A band of men on horses is coming over the hill!"

"Yes, I see them," said the king, holding his hand to his eyes and scanning the area. "Come, my son, let us ride quickly and find out what is going on," the king said, as he put his heel to his steed.

The closer they got, the more clearly they could see. There in the center of the square the people were fighting with hoe and pole, and a few were using bows and spears. They were being overwhelmed by the superior strength of the raiders. King Almar pulled his horse up to a halt, dismounted, and ran to the tower by the palace gate, with Mey at his heels. Almar took out his bow and began to shoot down the raiders. Mey tried to string a bow and help his father, but he could not get it right. His fingers felt clumsy and unskilled. A feeling of utter frustration came over him, and he broke the bow and threw it on the floor, with tears streaming down his cheeks. Mey had to stand by helplessly as the raiders returned their fire, until finally an arrow met its mark in his father's chest.

"Father," Mey yelled as he saw King Almar slump to the floor. He took his father in his arms, as his heart pounded and the perspiration ran down him in little rivulets. Mey sat there a long time holding his father until all was quiet again. Then he picked up King Almar and carried him down the stairs, for the king's heart was still beating and Mey knew he must get help. The raiders had left, and the bodies of the servants littered the courtyard. Mey felt the tears come to his eyes again at the sight of so much death and destruction, something he had never known before. He carried his father through the gates and into the palace. The few surviving servants ran to help him tend his father; they cleaned the wound in the king's chest and put him to bed. Then the long wait began for Mey. He never left his father's bedside once, while Almar lapsed in and out of consciousness.

Mey sat there for three days, in the depths of despair. Over and over he said to himself, "Worthless, yes, I was utterly worthless when my father needed me. The king wanted to teach me how to use the bow, but no, I was too lazy to put out the effort. Please, God, let my father live!"

At last he saw his father's eyes flutter open. "Father! Father! Thank God you're alive," Mey said as tears of relief rushed down his face. "It was my fault you were hurt, because I would not learn to use the bow. Forgive me, father."

"How long have I been asleep?" asked the king.

"Three days, my father," answered Mey.

"I have learned much while I was asleep," said Almar. "I know now that life is forever. I know that to be satisfied is not the way of growth. Before I knew no better, but I was wrong not to teach our people how to protect themselves. I should have made sure that you learned how to protect yourself and others, even if you did not want to. We will be prepared from now on, although we will hope never to have to use our knowledge. While I was asleep I remembered something my father showed me. Go now behind the throne room to the secret passage that I once showed you. Look there for a carved box with a sapphire eye on top. Hurry, my son, go and bring it back to me."

Mey asked no questions this time, but went and did as he was directed. He found the box easily enough and hurried back to the king. "Here it is, father," said Mey as he set it down before the king.

"Open it, please, for I am very weak," asked Almar. Mey opened the box and looked in wonder. There lay a magnificent sword. The glint of the blade made him blink, it was so bright. The handle was very ornate, and Mey noticed that it had once been set with jewels—many, many jewels as far as he could tell from the indented spaces.

"My father said his father once told him a story

about this sword," the king said excitedly. "I had forgotten, for at the time I never questioned."

"It is beautiful, father, but you should rest now and tell me about it later," pleaded Mey.

"There is no time for that, for I shall rest soon. I know that I only came back from my dream world to tell you about the sword. So listen to me carefully," said the king with authority. "This sword holds the secret of truth and power. But there is a missing part, which may be the jewels. I want you to take this sword and go out into the world to seek its secret, and to seek knowledge. When you have learned well, come home and teach our people. Do not let them dwell in ignorance any longer." The king looked long and deep into Mey's eyes as he said this.

"I will do as you bid, father, but you will not leave us yet," Mey said, the tears rolling down his cheeks. But as he looked, the king closed his eyes and returned to the world of his dreams.

Mey spent many days in deep sorrow at the loss of his father. He felt guilty for not having learned how to help him in his time of need, and he knew that he had not learned the art of bowmanship because he had not wanted to. But now he knew he would have to learn many things that he did not want to, things that he needed to know to help his people and fulfill his promise to his father. With these thoughts, Mey made a promise to himself that he would learn to use the bow, even though it was too late now to help King Almar.

It was now time to do as his father had bid him. Mey gave instructions to the people of the palace. He told them that he would be gone a long time; he had his saddlebags packed with food for himself and his horse, Kala; and in his loneliness with his bow and his sword, he set out on his quest for knowledge and the secret of the sword.

Chapter Seven

Mey Seeks

Not knowing where to go to seek knowledge, the first few days of Mey's journey through his father's land, which was now his, were spent in slow wandering from place to place. He stopped and talked to the people of the different villages, hoping someone would be able to direct him to the source of knowledge. He became very sad to see that all his people lived in ignorance, neither knowing nor caring to know.

He would have felt even more alone had it not been for his horse, Kala. Mey had raised Kala from the time he was a small colt. He had cared for him with gentleness and love, never breaking his spirit. Kala gave Mey complete obedience because of the love he had for him, and looking into Kala's eyes you could see the fire of his free spirit and the strength of his heart.

When they reached the border of their kingdom, Mey said to Kala, "Well, dear friend, we shall soon be coming to a new land. What we will find, we cannot even guess, for we have no knowledge of other places. All things will be new. But think, Kala, that is one way to learn. Everything we see and encounter will be an adventure." Mey reached over and gave Kala a loving pat or two, and Kala neighed in agreement.

At the end of their kingdom was a large plateau. Mey dismounted, led Kala to the edge, and both looked over to see what this next country was like. They saw before them a vast area of barren land, where the only vegetation seemed to be some bluish trees scattered far and wide. It was an ugly sight to Mey, who had come from a rich and fertile land, but to Kala he said, "Well, the only way we're going to find out about it is to go and see. Come, let us go on."

It took a long time for Mey to find a way down from the plateau. It seemed that no one had ever been this way before. But they wound their way down between the brush and the rocks and were finally on their way. They walked straight ahead, not knowing in which direction to go. They traveled all day and when they came to a small clump of the bluish trees, Mey decided that, since it was almost dark, they would camp there for the night. This was their first night alone. He was most grateful for Kala's

friendly neighing and snorting, which gave him a com-
forting feeling, and he slept.

Mey awoke to the first rays of the sun coming up,
and he marveled at the beauty of the sunrise. With no
vegetation on the plain, there was nothing to detract from
its beauty. "Kala, we will head into the sun, for east seems
to me to be the right direction. First let us eat and drink,"
he said. He took some bread and cheese for himself and
some oats for Kala out of the saddlebags.

As they were riding eastward Mey said, "It's funny,
but as I looked at the sun coming up I truly felt a sense of
direction. We shall keep walking east until we find what
we are seeking."

As they proceeded and the sun rose high overhead,
it became hot and sweltering. Now both Mey and Kala
found it hard to breathe. They finally came to a clump of
small trees. "Kala," whispered Mey, through his hot, dry
throat, "we had better stay here during the day and travel
at night. We haven't much water. There's a good fellow,
try to stay in the shade as much as you can and sleep."
Mey spread his blanket on the hot ground in the slight
shade cast by the trees, but he slept fitfully because of the
scorching heat.

When he awoke, he again admired the sun, which
was now setting. He saddled Kala, and so as not to tire
him, walked by his side. Mey walked a long time in si-
lence as the night grew darker. Impressed at the bril-
liance of the stars, he said to Kala, "Just look at the
untold millions of stars. Think of what there must be to
learn about them. Are there other worlds high above us?
If only we had someone to tell us the secrets of the stars."
The many questions that the stars brought to Mey's mind
kept him busy as they walked all through the night.

The sun rose again in the east, as now Mey knew it
would. He had learned many new things, and the things
he knew, he was sure of. Mey began to see an outline of
some hills far off on the horizon. "If we can reach those
hills, perhaps we can find water and food. We have only
enough to last for today," Mey thought as he looked
hopefully at the far-off hills.

That day passed and the next. Mey gave Kala the last
drop of water. He knew the horse required more than he

because he was so big. But after going without water, Mey was beginning to learn how precious it was. "Look, Kala! It's not much farther, perhaps half a day's journey," he thought to himself. He could not speak out loud to the horse, because his tongue was too swollen.

Mey could see trees and bushes at the foot of the hills, as the sun came up again. He wanted to hurry toward them, but he was too weak and could only stumble slowly onward. At last they were there, and they were overjoyed to find a spring with the sweetest, coolest water that either had ever tasted. After their thirst was quenched, exhaustion took over and they slept the whole day under a shade tree.

Mey awoke to the gnarling of his stomach. It had been almost three days since he had had anything to eat. He looked for Kala and saw him grazing on the grasses that grew by the spring. "Kala has found his food, now I must find mine," Mey thought. For the first time Mey had to rely on his own abilities to feed himself. Picking up his bow and arrows he walked carefully into the brush. Mey's skill with the bow was poor, and he spent a long time collecting his misguided arrows. But after many hours of frustration, he began to improve and feel more confident, and he finally came back to his camp proudly carrying a rabbit. Then he built a fire and cooked the rabbit, thanking the rabbit's spirit for letting him eat its body to sustain his own.

No longer hungry or thirsty, Mey began to feel much better, and he thought about the task of crossing the barren land. Suddenly he began to hear noises coming from the east; it sounded as though someone was coughing and choking. "Come, Kala," he said as he started saddling and loading the bags on his horse, "let's find out where that sound is coming from, and who is making it."

They made their way into the wooded part of the hills, and in the stillness of the night sounds carried a long way. Presently they came to a creek and followed it, and after a while they could make out some smoke and a little hut in a clearing by the creek. They made their way cautiously, for ever since the death of his father, Mey had learned to be cautious. He hid behind the trees as he came closer, and then he stopped in amazement. There, sitting by a small fire, was a very, very old man. His skin was taut against his bones, and he had an abundance of white hair, the purity of which was astonishing. Then Mey looked into his eyes. Despite his age, the old man's eyes had a brilliant sparkle.

Mey approached him respectfully and said, "Excuse me, but I heard you coughing and came to see who it was. May I be of help to you?" Mey had never seen anyone as old as this man.

Looking up at him, the old man said quietly, "I have been listening to you and your horse coming, since I had hoped I would not have to spend my last hours alone. Please sit with me, and tell me of yourself."

"My name is Mey and I am searching for knowledge," Mey replied, as he took his place on the other side of the fire.

"Your clothing is fine, like that of a prince," the old man said knowingly.

"I am a prince of another land, off to the west of here. My people live in ignorance, and when my father died he sent me to search for knowledge, so that one day I might return and teach them," answered Mey.

"There is no greater thing to seek after. I myself sought after knowledge and truth my whole life. You are right to try to find it and then use the good that you find. I never used what I found. I have much learning in my old head but I have never used any of it and now it is too late. There isn't even time to pass it on to you. I came here because I wanted to die where the sun sets, and think of all I have learned. When I listened to you, and heard that you wanted to learn in order to help your people, I realized that I have helped no one." The old man sighed and continued, "I will tell you what I can. Who knows, I may be able to use my knowledge at a later time."

"You speak of dying and yet also of a later time. What do you mean?" asked Mey.

The old man started coughing and was unable to stop for some time. Then he had to rest because the coughing had weakened him. Mey ran to the creek to bring him some water.

"Thank you," the old man said hoarsely, and remained silent for some minutes. Finally, he tried to answer Mey's question. "Young prince, did you leave your father's kingdom and arrive at my humble hut by taking just one step?" he asked.

"Oh no, old man," said the prince. "My horse and I must have taken thousands of steps, so many, in fact, that I grew so weary I thought we would die."

"Well, young prince," the old man went on, "life is a long journey too, longer than you think. What you call life is only one step in your total life. Man lives and dies and lives again many times. When a baby is born, a living being takes on a new form to complete another step in the long journey. What people call death is only a release from the old form used for this life. Very soon now, young prince, I will be free from this old form, to go on living without its restrictions. Yes, yes, very soon."

Mey sat still for some time in thought, and finally he said, "What you say seems true to me. When my father and I were learning together we planted some flower seeds. The flowers grew, blossomed, and died. But in the spring they grew again. Perhaps people are similar. I have a feeling there is much more."

"Go now and tend to your horse. Then come back and, if you will, prepare us both some supper," said the old man tiredly.

Kala snorted contentedly as Mey unsaddled him. He was very happy with the tender grass, and he knew that if he was being unsaddled they would not be doing any more traveling for a while. Mey brought his saddlebags over to the fire and set them down. "I am sorry, I have no food, but I can go out and hunt if you like," he told the old man.

"No need, no need," said the old man. "If you will go into the hut, you will find some dried grains to cook and some nuts and dried fruits. I brought enough supplies to last until it was time to go."

The meal was very satisfying to both, although the old man ate little. After Mey cleaned up, he sat down again to listen to what the old man had to say.

"Our meals taste much better when shared. Knowledge must be more pleasant too, when shared with another," sighed the old man.

"I have something here in my bag that I wish to share with you. Also, you may be able to tell me something of it, since you have so much knowledge," Mey said, as he reached into the bag and pulled out the box containing the sword.

The old man sat up even straighter when he saw the sapphire eye on the top of the box. "Ah, the eye, what a friendly sight," he murmured.

"My father gave me this sword," Mey said, as he lifted it gently out of its container. "He told me that it holds the secret of truth and power."

The old man looked in awe at the sword, and held his bony fingers out to touch it. Mey offered it to him, seeing that it gave him much pleasure.

"Indeed, this is the sword that I have heard of," exclaimed the old man, "but the jewels are missing—how sad."

"Yes, my father said that there was a missing part to the secret of the sword, which seemed to be the jewels," Mey said.

"I wonder if . . ." the old man paused, and then went on, "I wonder if the story I heard about a high priestess, who lives in a temple by the sea, is somehow connected with this sword."

"Please tell me what you have heard," pleaded Mey, becoming very interested.

"Well, there is not much to tell, simply that the high priestess was said to be the keeper of the jewels of knowledge and wisdom."

"Thank you. I feel that perhaps I should seek out and talk to this priestess. If she is the keeper of the jewels of knowledge and wisdom, who knows what I could learn from her," Mey answered gratefully.

Then the old man handed the sword back to Mey and admonished him sternly, "No matter what else you might have to part with in your travels, *never*, ever, part with this sword."

"I promise to let nothing but death come between me and the sword," Mey swore earnestly, happy that the old man had confirmed the importance of his father's gift to him.

"It will not be long before the dawn," said the old man, looking east.

"Forgive me, sir, I have been selfish in keeping you awake so long," said Mey apologetically.

"No, it is I who should apologize. I wish to share with you what I can before the dawn. With the coming of the dawn I shall depart from this old form," the old man said almost wistfully, "and I will ask you to do one thing for me, if you will."

"I will be happy to do whatever I can," Mey said, feeling sad that he must part so soon from his new friend, the first person of knowledge he had ever known.

"After all life has left this body, will you build a pyre and burn it, and let the ashes scatter where they will?" asked the old man.

This was a new custom to Mey. In his kingdom, the dead were buried in the ground, after much preparation. He asked the old man thoughtfully, "Burning a body will be a new experience for me. Will you please explain why you wish it?"

"I will be happy to tell you," said the old man, for each time he shared his knowledge with Mey, he felt happier and more contented. "This form we call a body is made up of all the elements of our planet. When we leave it at death, the elements begin to go their own way and the body falls to pieces. As this process starts, young prince, changes and new combinations of elements take place. During this period of transition, small animal life grows in the body to help in the transformation and many of the stages are dangerous to man's health. The cleanest and quickest way for the elements of the body to return to their source is through the purifying agency of fire. In very little time my body will be nothing but ashes; no one can be harmed by ashes, and the planet will be replenished."

"Will you tell me where you received all your knowledge?" Mey asked the old man. "I would be most grateful, for as I have told you, the search for knowledge is my quest."

"A quest, yes, my life was spent on the quest for knowledge," the old man said, thinking back. "One thing

I have learned, and for you to remember, is that knowledge is not just a collection of bits and pieces of information. To really know something you must prove it to yourself, either by experience or by knowing from within."

"But if someone has all the information, he could teach it to others, couldn't he?" questioned Mey.

"If you have not proven it to yourself, how are you to make others believe you?" replied the old man.

"Perhaps you are right," Mey said thoughtfully.

"Let me tell you where I found my knowledge," continued the old man. "I sought from everyone, until one day an old woman told me to seek out the four wisest ones on this planet—the wise one of the land, the wise one of the water, the wise one of the air, and the wise one of fire. I went through a great many trials for most of my life, but I found each one."

"How wonderful it must have been to talk to the wisest ones of the world," Mey exclaimed.

"Yes, and if I had more time I could tell you what I learned from each one, for I have spent all my last days thinking of such matters," sighed the old man.

"What was the most important thing you learned, if I may ask?" said Mey.

"I believe that the knowledge you find within your own being is more important and truthful to you than information from any other source. This is my most important belief, and I leave it with you, for now it is dawn. See, there comes the sun," the old man murmured softly, as he gradually relaxed his body and let it fall peacefully to the ground.

Mey jumped to his side, but it was no use. He leaned over to hear the heartbeat, but there was none. There was a peacefulness about the old man, and a soft smile on his lips.

Remembering what he had promised, Mey set about building a pyre on which to burn the body, which took him most of the day. He felt very tired, but content that he was able to fulfill the old man's last wish. He burned the body and let the winds scatter the ashes, glad that the old man was able to return to the elements of the planet so soon.

Packing his saddlebags, Mey felt as if he had lost

one of his best friends, although he had known the old man only one night. "Perhaps I have learned that time is not always necessary to establish a friendship," he thought.

As Mey and Kala rode away from the clearing and the little hut, Mey had many things to think about before he could decide in which direction to head. As he thought, he kept on going east.

He rode along, lost in his thoughts of the old man, until he realized that the terrain was changing. They were beginning to climb a range of low hills, each one a little higher than the last. Then suddenly Kala pulled to a halt. Mey awoke from his reverie and looked around him. Kala had stopped to admire a scene of glorious beauty. There in front of them were the highest mountains Mey could imagine. Mey had seen mountains before, but the mountains at home were not even half as high as these. These seemed to stretch up to meet the sky, and they extended to the left and right as far as the eye could see. Mey realized they would have to go down the hill and cross a green valley before they would reach the base of the fabulous mountains.

This was a good time and an excellent place to stop and rest from the morning ride. Kala ate grass and Mey ate some of the fruit from the old man's hut. Mey could not take his eyes off the glory of the mountains.

"I wonder what that white substance is, on the tops of the mountains?" he mused. "It seems to come only about a third of the way down. Well, I shall find out when we get there." Yes, the lure of these heights affected him now as those other mountains had when he was twelve. After their rest, Mey and Kala started out again. Now excitement ran through Mey's blood with the expectation of what lay ahead of them.

It took all day to cross the valley, so they spent the night at the base of the mountains. The night was warm and Mey watched the stars, always thrilled at the sight of a comet, before falling asleep.

Mey awoke at his usual time, but he could not see the sunrise because of the height of the mountains, which cast their shadow over most of the valley. He washed in the stream that ran by their camp, ate breakfast, and then mounted Kala and set off. It was a fairly easy climb for Kala, since the ground seemed to slope up gradually. On all sides evergreens and ferns grew in abundance. The air was cooler in these mountains than any air Mey had ever felt before, and he found the cool-ness and the fresh fragrance of the pines very pleasant. Finally it became too dark to go any farther, so they stopped and Mey built a fire. The night was cool. He bundled up with his blanket and curled up by the fire all night, and they set off again the next morning. Up and up and up they climbed. It was getting colder now, even when the sun shone on them. "Look, Kala," Mey yelled, "there's that strange white stuff we could see from the ridge! This means we are about two thirds of the way up."

Mey dismounted and went over to examine the strange white substance. He had never seen anything like it. He felt it; it was very cold. He smelled it; there was no smell. Then he tasted it and it tasted like water. "It seems like very cold water," he thought. "We will camp here, Kala," he called, "and go on in the morning." Mey built a bigger fire this time. He collected old dried wood so that he could keep the fire going during the night, deciding he did not like the cold. In spite of the cold Mey slept well most of the night, but from time to time he awoke and put more wood on the fire.

The next morning, after eating, he collected more dried wood and twigs with which to start a fire. He de-cided that if the white stuff was in fact a kind of cold water, then higher up he would not find dry wood be-cause he knew water made wood difficult to burn. He tied the bundle of wood onto the back of the saddlebags and they started into the snow. As they moved on, the white became deeper and deeper and it was slower going for Kala. The higher they climbed, the fewer the trees, until finally there were no trees at all. They stopped and rested and went on until Mey felt they were almost at the top. He could now see the view of the valley and hills from which they had come.

But suddenly the sky turned gray, and clouds seemed to envelop them as they reached the summit. White, cold water started coming at them from all direc-tions. Mey stopped and took his spare clothes out of the saddlebags and tied them to Kala's feet, for he felt sure they must be cold. He was very cold himself. Then he climbed up again on Kala's back, covered himself with the blanket, and let Kala have the lead. Mey could not see at all in the blinding whiteness, but he knew animals had a natural ability to find their way, so he felt he would have to trust in Kala. Everything was white—no depth, no direction, just white everywhere.

Mey had never seen snow before, and was afraid of the new coldness and intense whiteness. "What could this be?" he thought. "Where am I going? Poor Kala, he must be as cold as I am," and Mey's teeth chattered as he bent his frame into the wind. Suddenly Kala stopped and Mey nearly fell forward. Then he noticed the wind had stopped. Cautiously he peered out from beneath his blanket. To his astonishment, the whiteness was gone; now it was strangely dark on all sides. Cautiously Mey looked around him, and realized he was in a tall cave. He signed with relief. Kala must have seen the cave and walked right in.

Mey slid clumsily down from Kala's back and fell in an exhausted heap on the clean stone floor of the cave. He saw the storm raging outside, and, still shivering from the cold, he started shaking off the snow and Kala did the same. Suddenly he realized that there was a glow of light in the back of the cave. Mey got to his feet and stumbled toward the light. Rounding a slight bend in the wall of the cave he saw, to his astonishment, not an opening but an ancient figure seated on a rock, from whom the glow of light seemed to radiate. Mey was too awe-stricken to speak. He stood stock still. "I've never seen anyone as ancient as this. Am I dreaming?" he thought.

"No, you are not dreaming," spoke the ancient one. The sound seemed to press on Mey from all sides, all directions, gradually, until a shaking roar seemed to be coming from inside his own head. The voice came from everywhere, even from within. "And yes, I am indeed ancient. So ancient that when this land, this planet, was formed, I was here. Long ago, I watched and waited while the particles, built by the Father's helpers, were gradually pushed together by the force of light to form this orb, this planet. Again I had a home."

Mey was still standing in shock, but he ventured to ask timidly, "Who are you, sir? I am . . ."

"Welcome, Prince Mey," came the voice of the ancient one again. "I have trembled for you many times. I have waited long for you. Come closer, here beside me; I have much to show you. I know that your father sent you to seek knowledge, and I watched you with the old man at his hut. He was a good student of mine."

"Why, you must be one of the wise ones!" Mey exclaimed. "I hadn't dared hope to find one of you so soon."

"Some call me the wise one of the land," said the ancient one. "Of course, if they had been here as long as I have they would be just as wise." He laughed, and the sound seemed to shake the whole mountain.

"Good sir, may I ask how you saw me, across the great distance that is between here and the hut of the old man?" asked Mey very politely.

"Look over there," said the wise one, pointing at the opposite wall. "See those large crystals? That is how."

Mey saw many beautiful crystals, larger than himself and round like balls. They were perfectly clear with no imperfections. "They are very beautiful," said Mey.

"Watch now," said the wise one. The crystal nearest him started to form a cloudlike substance in its center, which spread throughout the crystal until it looked like smoke swirling—reddish-brown swirling smoke. The swirl of smoke began to grow smaller and more distinct, and a form appeared that was like a round ball Mey had played with as a child. The light which had been coming from all directions now seemed to come from only one direction. Gradually Mey began to feel he was being pulled into the scene in the crystal. The ball was getting nearer, or was he getting nearer the ball? Patches of green appeared on the now blue surface of the ball. As the scene came closer he could see that the green had a lot of brown and red, and that the blue was water. The patches were lands—changing, moving, disappearing. New lands replaced lost lands. Surface explosions spread red over parts of the land. Red entered the water and caused great clouds to rise. Somehow Mey knew. He knew this was the planet on which he lived, and he looked for his own kingdom.

Mey didn't have to wait long. The changes went by quickly. Soon a heart-shaped land appeared and he could see a long mountain range tearing through the heart. Then the scene grew dim and faded from view, and Mey heard again the wise one's voice, "You have just seen the birth of this planet, the Planet of Tears. Now come, look in this one, too," continued the voice surrounding Mey.

To the right of the faded crystal was another one, which grew cloudy as Mey began to stare into it. As the cloud cleared Mey saw the old man and himself talking and discussing the sword. Then a mist appeared and cleared, and Mey saw his father and himself in the library back at the palace. Mey thought his heart would break at seeing his beloved father, remembering again his feelings of failure and guilt at his father's death. Tears welled up in his eyes and everything became blurred. But the consoling thought came to him that he was already wiser and more responsible than he had been then. "And I will continue to learn!" he said to himself.

When Mey could see again, a beautiful, raven-haired girl stood before him. The scene behind her was a little fuzzy, but it seemed to be a temple of some kind. "Who is she?" stammered Mey. "I feel as though I know this girl. Ah, I know where I have seen her—in my dreams. I have dreamed about her, and in my dreams she seemed to belong with me somehow. Oh, how lovely she is!" Inspired by the vision, Mey began throwing questions at his host as fast as he could think—and that was very fast indeed.

"Listen now," said the wise one, "and I will answer some of your questions. In order for you to know that the birth of this planet was truth and not trickery, even though it was created millions of years ago, I had to show you things that only you could know, or things you thought only you knew. You see, Prince Mey, every event that has ever taken place is available for anyone who can attune to it. Nothing is ever lost, not even a single word spoken. That is one reason why what one speaks, or for that matter, thinks, is very important. Even what you call the future can sometimes be seen. Unless some drastic change is made in the pattern of events the future is predictable. Had you not interrupted me with your questions, I would have shown you an event in your future."

"I am sorry, wise one, is it possible to show me now?" asked Mey.

"I am sorry, it is only allowed to give you one demonstration. Once it was stopped it will not be continued." Seeing the disappointment on Mey's face, he went on, "Do not feel upset. It is not always good to see what is ahead. People sometimes wish to change an event that they think is a disaster, but that very event may be a part of their path to happiness, or to what they are seeking."

"Could you tell me . . ." Mey said hastily, but he was not allowed to finish.

"I remember your questions. Give me time and I will continue," the wise one said, kindly and matter-of-factly. "You did not really see the pictures in the crystals. The crystals were used as a point of concentration. You saw the pictures in your own inner eye. Yes, your thought is correct," the wise one continued, "the eye on the box represents the same inner all-seeing eye. I attuned myself with the scenes and projected them into your mind's eye. Now here is a real secret: although your body has a brain, your soul has a mind. This mind is an organ of perception, just as eyes and ears are organs of perception for your body. When you live as a soul that uses a body for a vehicle, and not as a body that is remotely connected to a soul, you have another organ with which to perceive throughout the vast reaches of the universe, regardless of time."

There was a long silence and the light in the cave grew as brilliant as full sunshine. Neither Mey nor the wise one noticed. Both had a far-off look in their eyes. Then Mey started to ask, "What about the . . . ?"

"Patience, my boy," interrupted the wise one. "The girl you saw lived at the temple. She is now the high priestess. But I don't know about your dreams. Only you will know that. When you find her, and I know you will search for her, you will know if she is the one of your dreams.

"Enough talk, it is late and you will want to start early in the morning when the weather is clear. If you take your blanket and lie next to your horse you will be warm enough."

It was then that Mey noticed there was nothing in the room but stone, rock, and crystal. He got up and bowed to the wise one, saying, "I am most fortunate and blessed to have met you, sir. Goodnight."

"It was a pleasure to welcome you, Prince Mey. Goodnight," said the wise one and bowed to Mey.

Mey went back out to where Kala was waiting. It did not seem so cold now. He had Kala lie down in the cave, and he curled up against Kala's warm body, covering them both with the blanket. It was quite a while before he slept, thinking about the wise one and what he had learned.

Mey awoke with the sun and jumped to his feet. Kala stumbled up also. Mey turned to go around the bend where the old man had been, but to his surprise he could see no opening, so he went to the wall and looked more closely. He felt the wall, but nowhere could he find an opening or see where there had been one. "Did I dream the whole thing?" he asked himself. "But it was too real to be a dream. I learned so very much, and I can remember it all so clearly, but why is there no opening?" In great confusion, Mey slowly saddled Kala and packed up his saddlebags, before the two of them left the cave to start their journey down the mountain.

Chapter Eight

Search

The air was crisp and cold as Mey and Kala stood admiring the spectacular view from the summit. The scene was almost as breathtaking as when Mey had first viewed the mountains. Looking down the mammoth work of art he was standing on, Mey thought about the creation of the planet he had seen in the crystal. "What a tremendous length of time it must have taken to create such magnificence," thought Mey. "What patience the creator must have." An immense vista lay open before him. He could see the small hills that extended from the mountain forests just below, out to the green valleys and then to the sea, which from this great distance was a deep blue and stretched as far as he could see.

Mey contemplated the wise one he had spoken with the night before. "I don't understand why I couldn't find him again this morning," he thought. "Perhaps I will understand at a later time. Does it really matter if I didn't find him again? What I learned was truth and reality to me.

"Now before the old man died he said that the high priestess, keeper of the jewels, lived in a temple by the sea. Last night the wise one said the girl I have dreamed of was the new high priestess. Are both the same, or am I looking for two different ones?" Mey began to realize that he had to find the priestess and the girl of his dreams, who were perhaps one and the same. Knowing what he was searching for and where he was headed again gave Mey a surge of excitement.

Kala and Mey made their way rapidly down through the snow, which was not as deep on this side where the morning sun kissed it each day, and before mid-morning they reached the snow line. Sitting down on a tree stump, Mey ate some of the fruits and nuts that were left, while Kala grazed on some grasses that grew among the trees.

Halfway down the slope they came to a path, which showed some evidence of being well-traveled, so the journey downhill became easier for Kala. His legs were tender from the rough ice they had gone through before reaching the summit the night before.

Nearing the base of the mountain, Mey rode along tranquilly, letting his thoughts drift with the scenery. But all of a sudden he was jerked roughly to the ground. As he felt himself hit the hard soil, he heard Kala give a wild snort. Shaking his head to clear his vision, Mey tried to get up, but was violently pushed back. A strong, repugnant odor reached him as he looked into the faces of the dirtiest, meanest looking men he had ever seen, leering and grinning down at him. Standing directly in front of him was a man who seemed to have a fair complexion, but he was so dirty that Mey could not tell for sure. Next to him was a man so black he was almost blue. Mey got slowly to his feet, aching and bruised. "What can I do for you?" he said, trying to force an air of dignity, although in reality he was shaking inside with fear.

"Hear that, fellows?" grunted the blond man. "This young lad wants to know what he can do for us." With that, they all laughed heartily.

"Then I shall be on my way," Mey said, trying not to show how frightened he was, "if you will kindly turn loose my horse." His words were greeted with uproarious laughter again. Two men clung tightly to the horse's reins to prevent Kala from running over to Mey's side.

"Where do you keep your gold and jewels?" the dark man asked Mey.

"I have none," answered Mey truthfully.

"Search him and his saddlebags," shouted one of the bandits, with a voice like gravel.

Two of the men searched Mey roughly, looking for anything of value, while others went through the saddlebags. They found nothing but the box containing the sword.

"Is this all you have? A richly dressed lad like you, who owns such a fine horse," grunted one of the bandits. If any man could look meaner than the first two Mey had seen, this one did, with his lip curled up in a snarl. He opened the box greedily and took out the sword. "It's a handsome sword, but what about its jewels?" said the man. "Well, let's see what kind of use we can make of it." He held the sword by the hilt and hefted it in his hand. It felt heavy and without balance. He took a swipe or two at a nearby bush, but there was no edge to the sword. "Even your sword is no good," he snarled. "Here, you can have it back. It would be worthless as a weapon."

Mey leaned down, picked up the sword, and held it

in his hand. "Perfect balance," he thought. It felt good in his hand; it felt powerful. As he slowly turned it, the sun shone on it, and he saw the same shiny edge he had seen when his father had first opened the box. "I wish I knew how to use you, sword of power," Mey thought. "What can I do to defend myself against these bandits? Nothing."

"Well, lad, we can at least make use of your horse," one of the men said as he raised a whip and brought it down hard on Kala's back. "I'll soon break his ornery spirit," he snarled.

"Take your filthy hands off my horse," Mey yelled, grabbing the sword firmly and starting toward Kala. In his rage Mey forgot his fear.

"You want to fight us, eh?" laughed one of the men. "Look at him, fellows, he wants to fight us with his pretty little sword. Shall we give him a chance?" They all laughed in agreement.

"I'll make short work of you," said one with a horrible grin, as he came at Mey with a long curved knife.

Mey stood back, sweat breaking out on his forehead and the palms of his hands. "Well, now what shall I do?" he thought. "They might kill me and still take Kala. Why have I let my anger cause this? Now I am forced into fighting and I don't even know how." The man advanced slowly toward him. Somehow—Mey never knew how—he blocked the knife that came at him and with a loud clang he cut the knife in half. All the bandits looked on in astonishment. How could a sword with no edge do such a thing? Then their anger came flooding back. They all grabbed their weapons and rushed at Mey, letting go of Kala as they did so. As each man attacked, Mey destroyed his weapon with a blow of his sword. Mey felt as if he were moving in a dream. He was moving very fast, since more than one bandit was coming at him now. As he disarmed each one, Kala wildly chased after the bandit, rearing and kicking. Soon the boy and his horse began to triumph and the bandits began to give up, although they outnumbered Mey ten to one. Mey swung his sword at each one, lopping their swords to pieces, and Kala raged around after each one like a wild beast gone mad. Finally the last bandit ran off in fright, and Mey and Kala were left alone and out of breath. Mey sat down in exhaustion, while Kala stood over him protectively.

"What a friend you are, Kala," Mey said, regaining his breath and looking lovingly up at his horse, "and what a sword! What power! I had the strange feeling that the sword was doing everything by itself. Oh, how I wish my father could have seen us." Then Mey started laughing so hard that he rolled on the ground holding his sides. "How funny we must have looked," he said as he looked up at Kala, still laughing.

After resting for a while, Mey decided to move on. He was grateful for being spared and realized it was unwise to take unnecessary chances. He decided to try to get to the valley he had seen from the summit.

But the valley was much farther away than Mey had thought, and by nightfall they had reached only the foothills. "Kala," Mey said, "we are both tired. We will camp here for the night." They bedded down in a clearing where they had a clear view of anyone approaching them. They slept so soundly, completely worn out from their long day of traveling and their battle with the bandits, that had anyone come into their camp, they would never have awakened.

The next morning they set out again, and Mey started talking to Kala. He felt as if Kala understood everything he told him. No love between animal and man could match the feeling that Mey and Kala had for each other. "Kala," Mey said, "I had a dream about that girl again last night. This time it was a wedding of some kind between her and myself, which took place in a strangely designed building. The love and oneness I felt is indescribable, even to you my friend of all friends. If she exists anywhere outside of my own mind, we must find her. Perhaps she will be at the temple when we find it."

At the bottom of the foothills they came to a small town that looked like many of the small towns in Mey's land. Mey dismounted and made his way confidently into the center of town. Walking by Kala's side, he watched the townspeople scurrying here and there doing their daily business, paying no attention to him. He stopped a man on the street and asked for directions to the governor; the man told him to go the largest house at the end of the street. On reaching the house, Mey walked up to the door and knocked boldly. A heavy-set woman of middle age answered the door, peering out to see who was there. "Excuse me for troubling you, but I am looking for the governor of this town. I was told that he lives here," Mey said nervously.

"He does," the woman answered bluntly. "Wait here, and I will go to find him." With that she shut the door. A little taken aback at her rudeness, Mey waited, and after some minutes the door opened again. There, looking up at him, stood a man with intense eyes that took in every detail of Mey's appearance in a rapid, searching glance. He was a short round man with a round head—bald except for some white hair sticking out by his ears. "I am the governor of this town. May I be of service to you?" he said.

"Perhaps you can, good sir," replied Mey. "I am traveling through your land in search of a temple by the sea. Could you be so kind as to tell me if you know of such a temple? If so, could you give me directions on how to get there?"

Looking Mey over thoroughly, the curious little man could tell by his mannerisms and clothes that here was nobility of some kind. "Yes, I think that I might be of some help to you. Won't you come in and rest from your journey, and tell me from where you came?" he said, for he enjoyed company, especially important company.

"I would be honored," answered Mey. "I will first unsaddle my horse so that he might rest also." Mey hurriedly unsaddled Kala and, his heart pounding at the hope of finding the temple, went into the man's house.

Mey introduced himself to his host, saying, "I have come across the high mountains and before that, the barren land. On the other side of the barren land is my kingdom, the land of King Almar. Excuse me for looking so disheveled, but I ran into bandits in the forest."

"I am known as Arn," said the governor with a pleased look on his face. He had never had such important company before. The woman who had answered the door came in with refreshments. Sweetmeats, fruit, bread, and wine were served to Mey and his host. The woman was most pleasant and eager to please now that she had overheard that she was serving a prince.

As he ate in silence, enjoying every bite, Mey thought about how differently people treated him when they knew he was a prince. "Am I not the same person, prince or no prince?" he thought. "Is a title what counts, or the person himself?"

Finishing his meal some time before Arn, Mey tried to appear absorbed with his wine, not wanting to make his host uncomfortable. Arn ate and drank until there was nothing left on the serving plates. Mey could see why he was fat. Arn was not only prideful, but entirely self-indulgent. When he had drunk the last drop of wine, swallowed the last sweetmeat, and wiped his face with his shirt sleeve, Arn spoke, "In this land, it is the custom for every village or town to send one or two youths, male or female, to the Temple of the Sun to serve our gods. The governor of the town escorts them there. It has been many years since the last time I was there, and it will be at least another five years before I go again. I myself do not like to get too close to the gods."

Pleased to hear of the temple at last, and eager to learn its location, Mey again asked Arn, "Would you please tell me how I might find the temple?"

"If you keep directly east of here, you will find it. The temple sits on a bluff overlooking the sea," replied Arn. Arn wished to keep his guest as long as he possibly could, since no one else in town had ever had a prince to entertain, and he looked forward to all he would have to boast about the next day. "It's about three days away by horse. Meanwhile I would be most honored if you would stay the night in my humble house," he said, a smile coming to his lips as he bowed to Mey.

"Since it is growing late in the day, I will be very happy to stay, if it does not inconvenience you," said Mey.

"On the contrary, you do me great honor," replied Arn.

Grateful for the luxury of sleeping in a bed and enjoying his full stomach, Mey retired for the night, placing his sword close by his side. Since his encounter with the bandits, Mey was careful to keep the sword close by him at all times.

Mey woke once during the night with a strange dream, in which a thick blanket of fog was enveloping him so tightly he couldn't breathe and eyes seemed to be looking right through the fog at him. But this passed and he slept the rest of the night peacefully.

On arising, Mey was anxious to be on his way, now that he knew where to find the temple. "If it is the right one, perhaps my search will be over," he thought as he dressed. Then he reached for the sword. "My sword!" he called out in alarm. The sword was not there. He looked everywhere in the room, and the more he looked, the more frantic he became. "It's gone, it's really gone," Mey called out in despair.

There was a knock on the door. Mey opened it and there stood Arn, his eyes open wide. "I heard you shout, dear prince. Is anything wrong?" he said.

"Yes, the sword I had with me is gone. Do you know who could have taken it?" Mey asked in desperation.

"No, are you sure it is gone?" Arn's concern seemed to be genuine. "I didn't hear anyone enter or leave the house. Here, let me help you look again." And Arn began searching the room, but he found nothing either. Arn called out a search party, and every house and building was searched, but to no avail. The sword was nowhere to be found.

"I am so sorry your sword could not be found," Arn said with head bowed. "I did hear that a stranger came into town very late last night, and is gone today. Some say he was one of the servants of the dark lord who rules some distance from here."

"Tell me of this lord," Mey asked.

"I know very little, I'm afraid," said Arn. "It is said that he never leaves his kingdom, that he sends his servants to do his evil bidding far from home. I have heard people say that if you enter his land and are lucky enough to return, you will never forget the horror of what you have seen there, and in the end you will lose your mind." Arn paused, and then asked, "What will you do now?"

"There is not much I can do but go to the temple. Perhaps I will find some help there," replied Mey in a low voice, but inwardly he was thinking, "I promised to let only death come between me and the sword. Why would someone take it? Who is this dark lord? Father, I've failed you again." These thoughts hung heavy on Mey.

They set off for the temple with a heavy heart and traveled for four days. Kala walked slowly, feeling the weight of his master's sadness. Late in the afternoon the outline of the temple buildings came into view. "There it is, Kala!" Mey said, some of his enthusiasm returning.

When they came close enough to see clearly, Mey's heart seemed to leap to his throat. The stone walls were still standing, but the rest was gone, destroyed by fire. "Who could have done this?" Mey asked in bitter disappointment. Dismounting from his horse, he sat on the worn temple steps with his head in his hands. "Is this the end of my search for the priestess?" he cried. Mey looked at Kala and there were tears in his eyes. Getting up and looking at the temple with his blurred vision, he was certain that this was the same temple he had seen in the crystal. He thought about the beautiful girl of his dreams. Was she destroyed also? Mey began searching through the ruins and the gardens, noticing that they were still well kept. "It hasn't been long since the disaster by the looks of this," thought Mey, but the thought made him feel even worse. "If only I had been able to get here sooner, I might have been able to help."

Suddenly a voice interrupted his thoughts. "What do you want here?"

Turning around, Mey saw a man in a white robe. "I came to see the high priestess of this temple," Mey answered.

"She was murdered when the temple was destroyed," the man replied, a great sadness showing in his face.

Mey slumped down in despair. So this was the end of his search, the priestess was dead. The man in the white robe came over and sat beside him to comfort him.

"Can you tell me what happened, and how long ago it was?" Mey asked, feeling a strange desire to know the details.

"I was one of the temple helpers here," began the man. "I have been here since I was a youth. I was happy and content here, as most of us were. Yet when the raiders came, I and another ran and hid, instead of trying to help protect the priestess." He stopped for a moment as sorrow overwhelmed him; Mey was the first person he had been able to tell of his grief. He continued in a low voice, "When we came back, after the raiders left, there were only the two of us and Treaia still alive. Treaia had been far away down the beach when it happened. She found Ramana, who was our high priestess, still alive, and Ramana gave Treaia some jewels and sent her on a search of some kind. After we took care of the bodies, Treaia told us we could go where we liked. I stayed here."

"Tell me more of this Treaia, please," Mey said, with a feeling of hope.

"Treaia was Ramana's temple daughter. When Ramana died, she became high priestess of the sun," the helper answered, shaking his head regretfully.

"Please tell me what Treaia looks like," Mey pleaded.

"Oh, about your age, lad, very lovely, with dark hair and ivory complexion. For one still so young, she is very wise. Now that Ramana is gone, Treaia is most likely the wisest in the land. She was trained to be so. When I think of how happy and full of merriment she was, it is hard to remember the look on her face as she left," the helper said, as a far-off look came to his eyes and he remembered happier times. The weight of sadness was lifted off Mey's heart as he listened. He felt sure that Treaia and the girl of his dreams were one and the same. "Where has she gone? Please show me the way. I must find her," Mey said, taking the man by the shoulders.

The temple helper could not understand this new look of happiness on the young man's face, but he was happy to point out the way. "She left in the direction of the primitive village; it was the closest place. But it has been some time since the day she left."

Mey thanked him and ran to Kala, saying, "Let us go! She is alive! We must find her!" They rode for several hours until Mey realized it had grown dark. "I am sorry, my friend," he said to Kala, as he stopped and got off his horse. "In my impatience, I forgot how long you have carried me this day. We will rest the night here."

With the help of Kala, Mey arrived at the village much more quickly than Treaia had. He dismounted and walked into the village, hoping to find her there. "I have never seen a town or village as primitive as this," he thought, gazing around him in surprise.

The villagers were cowering in fear, peeking out from behind their doorways and from behind the trees. Not knowing quite what to do, Mey waited in the hope that someone would come out to welcome him. But finally he grew tired and spoke up. "Kind people," he called, "is Treaia here?" No answer. He tried again. "I am looking for the high priestess of the temple. Is she here?" With these words, the toothless old chief walked slowly up to Mey. He was shaking with fear because he, like all the other people in the village, had never seen a horse before. The only horse he had heard tell of belonged to the evil lord of the forest, of whom his hunters had told him many terrible tales. But he also knew that the priestess had entered the forest. "Perhaps this is the evil lord?" he wondered. "But why is he looking for her, if she went into his forest? This lord must be a different lord." These and many more terrifying thoughts went through the old chief's head. Trembling, he said, "I am chief here, so only I may speak with you. What is it that you want with the priestess?"

"I wish to speak with her," replied Mey softly, not wishing to frighten the old man.

The chief had worked himself into such a fright that out of his mouth rushed a torrent of words, "Please, oh god, do not punish us. We have already suffered enough from the god of storms and the god of the birds who came upon us. The priestess was not harmed. She fled into the forest." Dropping to his knees, he begged for mercy from this new god with the fearful beast.

Looking down on this pitiful sight, Mey said to the chief, "Get up, old one, I will not harm you. Tell me what you did to make the priestess flee from this village."

Grateful that his life was spared, the chief rose to his feet with difficulty, and began telling Mey his story. "We thought it was her fault that the god of storms came upon us. But, before the sacrifice could take place," he motioned toward the altar, "all the birds of the land came at us. Then the priestess fled toward the forest," he pointed out the direction, "and we have not seen her since."

Mey climbed up on Kala's back in silence and headed south, the direction the chief had pointed out. For the first time Mey realized he was no longer traveling east. He was facing into the full warmth of the southern sun, and had been ever since he had left the temple.

Chapter Nine

Mey Meets Tartek

Treaia—now he knew her name. "How sweet the sound of it is," he thought, as he and Kala continued on their way. Consumed with the idea of finding her and lost in daydreams, Mey had no thought of caution.

Suddenly Kala shied back, nearly unseating Mey. A dark, slithering, loathsome something moved across their path; a freezing chill ran down Mey's spine; and Kala refused to move. Mey looked around the forest for the first time since they had entered it, and began to sense an odd difference. He noticed that the trees were twisted and gnarled and entangled with one another, unlike the straight tall pines of other forests. As he looked, he listened. It was very quiet. No familiar sounds came to his ears. The only noises he could faintly discern were strange sounds of groaning and wailing.

"That was the strangest thing I have ever seen," Mey whispered to Kala. "It was so loathsome that my curiosity cannot even persuade me to follow it. But we must go on and search for Treaia. Let us proceed with great caution from now on. It is getting late, and we will soon have to stop for the night." Mey kept talking to Kala, because the forest made him nervous. Both were looking forward to reaching the end of the forest. "Look, over there to our right is a light!" cried Mey in relief. Turning Kala in that direction, he made his way over the tree stumps and in between the tangled trees. "It's a cottage, and a very charming one, too," Mey said, glad to have found a friendly place to spend the night. He went up to the door and knocked loudly.

"May I help you?" said a sweet voice as the door opened. Standing there before Mey was a young girl about his own age, with fair skin, soft brown hair flowing to her waist, and large, doelike, brown eyes. She smiled at Mey and said politely, "Won't you come in? You must have come a long way to find my little cottage." She held the door open wide for her guest.

Pleased to find someone at home and charmed by her beauty and sweet nature, Mey stepped inside. "Thank you, miss. My name is Mey. How kind of you to invite me into your home," he said, bowing low.

"And my name is Mira," she said, taking him by the hand and leading him over to a seat in front of the fire.

103

The room glowed pleasantly, warming Mey's heart. "Sit here and rest, I will tend to your horse and bring back refreshments," said Mira; giving Mey no time to refuse, she quickly left the room.

"How lovely and how thoughtful Mira is," Mey thought, settling himself in the chair and feeling very relaxed. He felt so warm and comfortable that he fell asleep. But in his dreams Treaia's voice seemed to be saying to him, "Beware, beware."

"Good morning, Mey," Mira said as she stood over him. "You were so tired last night that I covered you and let you sleep."

"How kind you are, Mira," said Mey, jumping to his feet. "Will you show me where I may wash?"

Mey enjoyed his breakfast and the company of Mira. She was quick and witty in her conversation, and Mey laughed more than he had in many weeks. "Tell me why a young woman like yourself would live alone in the middle of this forest?" he asked her.

Laughing gently and throwing back her hair to show her graceful neck, she answered, "There are several reasons. One is that I enjoy the loveliness of the wildlife and being alone with my thoughts. Another is that a wise man once told me that if I were to go and live in the thick of the forest, one day my true love would come and find me." She blushed with these last words, and turned away from Mey coyly. "And you, why are you here in the forest?" she asked.

"I am searching for a girl named Treaia, and I was told she came this way," Mey answered.

"I have never seen or heard of a girl by that name," Mira said innocently. "Are you sure you are looking for the right girl?" Before Mey could answer, she jumped up and grabbed his hand, saying, "Come with me and I will show you my gardens."

Her trees and flowers were very different from the ones Mey had seen the night before. Here there were lovely little paths, along which grew flowers and ferns. Soon they came to a spring flowing over a waterfall. Pulling Mey down beside her, Mira asked, "Do you see why I enjoy living in these woods?"

"Yes, it's lovely here around your cottage," Mey answered, allowing her to pull his head down into her lap. As her fingers stroked his hair, Mey thought this the most pleasant day he had ever spent. "Treaia was just a dream after all," he thought, "only a dream. But Mira—she is flesh and blood, and surely no one could be more gentle and sweet than she."

"It is almost dusk, Mey," Mira said. "Let us go and have supper, and sit before the fire this evening."

Feeling pleasantly relaxed after a nice supper, Mey was enjoying sitting before the fire with Mira at his side. This time Mey reached over and took Mira's hand in his. Treaia and his search were gone from his thoughts. Mira was soft and yielded to the touch of his hand. He bent over her and placed his lips on hers. With his eyes closed, feeling the tingling of his lips meeting the softness of hers, Treaia's face flashed before his closed eyes. The pain made his heart tighten into a hard lump. "What am I doing?" he thought, as he started to pull himself away from Mira. "I am very sorry for what I did," he said to Mira, but he found to his surprise that he could not move. Mira was clasping him tightly with her arms around his neck. Mey pushed her back in fear and looked into her face. There, in the place of pretty Mira, was a hideous-looking hag with drooping, sagging skin, and teeth missing. Her hair had turned gray and she laughed maliciously, still hanging on to him tightly.

"You are to be my love, and I will never let you go," Mira said, letting out a shrill scream.

Mey's head began to swim with the terror that he felt and the horror that was locked around him. Summoning all the strength he had, he pulled away from her and ran to the door. He found Kala, saddled him as quickly as possible, and rode off, all the while hearing the shrill cackling coming from the cottage.

The trees again became twisted and gnarled, and Kala made his way as swiftly as he could, sensing his master's terror. After some time had gone by, Mey calmed down and could speak again. "I can't understand. I cannot even imagine what took place back there in the cottage with Mira," he told Kala. He reached over and patted Kala, for it gave him comfort, and went on telling him about his ordeal. Mey rode on, thinking that he must be going mad, as the hideous peals of laughter rang through the night.

Too tired to go any farther, Mey and Kala stopped to rest. Mey stretched out in the most comfortable spot he could find, with his head resting on a large root that protruded from the ground. He was just beginning to fall asleep when he heard Kala whinny and screech. Mey jumped up and, to his horror, by the light of the feeble moon he saw Kala totally encircled by a terrible serpent that covered his entire body, except for his eyes. The serpent had a large head, and its forked tongue was striking viciously at Kala's eyes. Mey's first impulse was to run; fear struck his heart when he saw this monstrous snake. But looking into Kala's eyes and seeing his friend's terror, Mey swallowed his own fear, knowing his responsibility to Kala. "What could I use to destroy this monster?" he thought. "If only I had the sword. There's my bow and arrows, but my aim is unsure. Could I possibly hit the snake without injuring Kala? I could make a club out of an old limb of a tree. But would that do it?"

Mey was torn, trying to think what to do. Finally, he decided the arrow would be best. "Oh God, make my aim sure just this once," he prayed. As Mey took a deep breath, he was frightened and unsure, but he drew back the bow and aimed at the serpent's head. As he let the arrow go he pleaded, "Please, God, let me save Kala and I will practice the bow until I am an expert." The arrow went straight and true into the head of the serpent. In relief, Mey wiped his forehead with his arm and went over to Kala. The serpent was dead but its long body was still entwined around the horse. Mey shuddered as he began the task of releasing him. Free at last, Kala nuzzled Mey in gratitude, and both tried to settle down to sleep for the rest of the night.

However, when dawn came to the forest, there was no sunrise; the light merely changed from black to gray. "Kala," Mey said, "I still don't understand what has been happening, but I'm sure that this is en evil forest. Let's keep moving as fast as we can. It will be a blessing to be out of here."

Meanwhile, Tartek was watching what was going on

from his castle. "Treaia," Tartek grunted, "so that's what he's after. But if I can't have her, nobody shall. Well, he will never leave my forest. He's the best sport I've had for a long time. He really fell for my little Mira, and for my serpent."

As he spoke, Tartek was swinging a sword, trying to get the feel of it. "I don't understand. This is supposed to be a powerful sword, but it has no balance or sharp edge. Even the hilt feels crude where the jewels used to be. Perhaps my servants stole the wrong sword. This one is worthless." Tartek threw the sword back into its box in disgust.

He went to dress for company, since he could see Mey coming toward the castle from a long way off. "Now," he thought, "I'll be able to find out why Mey is searching for Treaia."

"Look, Kala," Mey said, as he saw a grand castle coming into view. The trees had changed again and were stately and tall. "Maybe this is the end of the evil forest."

As Mey and Kala rode up, the gates of the courtyard were opened for them. "Is your master home?" Mey inquired of the servant.

"Yes, my lord," said the servant. "If you will come this way, I will present you."

Mey followed the servant into the wide reception room, in the middle of which stood Tartek, dressed in regal fashion. He spoke in a most eloquent voice. "I am Tartek. What can I do for you, good sir?"

"I've never seen such a handsome man," Mey thought. To Tartek he said, "I have just passed through the dark forest, my lord, and I am looking for a girl. She is called Treaia. Perhaps she has passed this way?"

Just then another servant entered the room and announced that lunch was to be served.

"Come, join me for lunch and we shall talk," Tartek said, as he led Mey into the dining room. "You haven't told me your own name yet."

"Forgive me, I am called Mey," Mey answered politely.

As their meal was being served Tartek asked in a concerned fashion, "Tell me of this girl you are seeking."

So Mey told him everything he knew of Treaia. "I

even dream of her; whenever I close my eyes I see her face," he added as he reached the end of his story. In surprise, Mey watched Tartek's eyes grow cold and his mouth twist up into an ugly sneer.

"I have some important business to take care of. Please make yourself at home and I will return soon," Tartek said, hastily leaving the room. The thought of someone else desiring what he himself desired caused Tartek to start shaking in an uncontrollable rage. Wild with hate, he stormed off to plan Mey's destruction and regain his calm and deceptive exterior.

Mey arose, feeling uneasy, as his host left the room. "Why did Tartek become so upset when I spoke of Treaia?" he asked himself. "He has yet to tell me if she has been this way. I'm sure that something is wrong. But what did Arn tell me about an evil lord? The forest I have just passed through was certainly evil; could this elegant gentleman possibly be the evil lord himself? It doesn't seem possible. In many ways he's so charming. I'll ask about Treaia again when he returns."

Having decided this, Mey started looking over the room, finding much pleasure in the beauty of it. His natural curiosity soon led him to the next room, and then the next. As he looked around, his eyes suddenly fell on the box with the sapphire eye. "He is the evil lord!" Mey whispered hoarsely. "And here is my sword," he cried, opening the box and looking in.

In panic, Mey snatched up the box and stealthily made his way back through the rooms and out of the castle. Finding the stable, he hurriedly saddled Kala and rode out of the courtyard as quickly as he could.

"Look at the young fool run—as if he could elude me," Tartek muttered maliciously, as he watched Mey from his window. A peal of sinister laughter escaped from his throat.

Mey rode hard, trying to find his way out of Tartek's kingdom, but it seemed to be never-ending. As he rode, he heard Tartek's voice echo all around him, "You shall never leave here alive. You shall never follow Treaia."

"What does he know about Treaia?" Mey yelled to the wind.

Suddenly Kala pulled up short—a raging wall of fire had appeared in the distance. There was no way to turn, except back. "Back to what?" thought Mey in despair. "Did Treaia go through all this horror also? Treaia, Treaia," he said to himself, "how little I know of you. Did you suffer also? And how little I know of myself! Until now I have thought only of my own search, my own desires. I pray that I will be given strength to face what will come, the trials I must surely endure. But now I see that this search means more to me than the gratification of my own desires.

"I started seeking knowledge for myself, but I must really seek it for Treaia also and for my people. I had forgotten about my people, forgotten why I had first started looking for Treaia. What came over me? My search for Treaia was passionate and personal only, with no thought for her or for my people. I see, Kala, that something was wrong with the way I used my feelings and passions. I will try to learn to recognize and use them in a proper way."

Then Mey was torn away from his thoughts by the sound of breaking branches crashing to the ground, followed by a deep roll of thunder. A nine-headed beast, eyes blazing and long tongues flickering fire, was racing toward him. These nine heads were joined to a trunk from which extended eighteen stout leathery legs, terminating in hoofs that struck sparks from the rocks. A wave of nausea spread over Mey as he watched the hideous creature prepare to charge at him. Then Mey saw his adversary, Tartek, riding immediately behind the beast, standing firmly as the wheels of his chariot churned up the earth.

Tartek circled around and around Mey and Kala, laughing insanely. Kala became wild with terror, stumbling and throwing Mey to the ground, and with him the box and the sword. The box fell open as it hit the ground. Mey grabbed the sword, clambering back to his feet in confusion.

"You are as worthless as your sword," laughed Tartek, turning his beast around to make the final charge. "I am tired of this game—I shall end it now."

Tartek's voice rang in Mey's ears. "Worthless sword, that's what the bandit said too," thought Mey. "Is it worthless? It has served me well once. It has more power than Tartek thinks."

Coming at them at full speed were Tartek and the nine-headed beast. Mastering all the courage he had, Mey side-stepped to the right and swung the sword at the last head. A blaze of light appeared as the sword cut off the head.

Tartek cursed, turned the beast, now with only eight heads, and came at Mey again. To Mey's horror, he saw that the beast had regrown the ninth head. "What chance do I have against this?" Mey thought in terror as he again slashed at the nearest head and ran out of the way of the trampling hoofs. Again he saw the brilliant light, which left the creature with only eight heads.

Once more Tartek turned his beast around, cursing, "You cannot destroy *my* creation. Now you shall die."

Out of breath and wiping his wet palm on his side, Mey took a firmer grip on the sword. He watched the beast grow another head as Tartek made his wide turn. "How is this possible?" thought Mey. "Tartek just said that the beast is his own creation and I could not destroy it. Why? But didn't the ancient wise one tell me about pictures in the mind? Could that be it? How could my mind allow Tartek to produce such a horrific creature? But Mira changed from a pretty girl into an ugly hag. Desire and ugliness, it must have something to do with desire and ugliness."

Mey thought rapidly; the beast seemed to have grown even larger. Tartek and the beast had made the turn and were thundering down on him, the wall of fire still raging behind them.

Mey tried to run out of the way once again, but caught his foot in a bush. Tartek and the beast were upon him. "Is this the end?" thought Mey, but at the same time he began to feel the warming strength of his new understanding of the beast and he plunged his sword deep into its heart. With a blinding flash of light the beast reared up, throwing itself to the ground and Tartek out of his chariot. When Mey finally dared to open his eyes, the beast and the wall of flame were gone. Only Tartek remained, lying unconscious on the ground. Mey picked up his sword, once again overwhelmed with gratitude for its power.

Mey had no memory of mounting Kala and riding out of the forest. His next conscious recollection was of Kala's wet neck pressed to his face and arms, as the horse ran and ran, leaving the evil forest far behind them.

Chapter Ten

Mey Meets Treaia

Meanwhile, after waking from her strange delirious dream, Treaia found her fever gone and heard the sweet melody of the birds singing a welcome to a new day. Hearing the birds, Treaia knew she was at last out of Tartek's reach. In the forest of deception there had been no birds. She went and bathed in the lake, splashing the refreshing liquid over herself, smiling as she remembered her dream about the lake. Feeling better but still very tired from her long run and delirium, Treaia looked around and found a soft grassy spot under a tree, and slept. A peaceful deep sleep came over her, the kind that lets the voice of knowing slip in. During her sleep, she had a dream.

"My daughter," spoke a voice, "when you awake, keep traveling south until you come to a little village by the sea. Stay there until the one with the sword finds you."

On waking, Treaia wondered about her dream. "Does the one of my dreams really exist? The voice I heard spoke with such authority. I will do as the voice said," she said to herself. So Treaia made her way south, eating berries and roots as she went. At night she slept in the open under the stars, and she would wake to the singing of the birds.

The forest was now behind her and the rolling hills of green stretched before her, with the high mountains to the west. The smell of fresh salt air soon made its way to her nostrils. "The smell of the sea—oh, how I love it," she thought. "It reminds me of the temple. The sea always seems to have an adventuresome and free spirit. At first it's quiet and inactive, then it swells into majestic activity. During the quiet, still times, the sea seems to be resting, contemplating its next exciting adventure. It's like watching life in motion."

As Treaia walked to the crest of the hill, she caught her first view of the fishing village. It was a nice looking village with little houses, which were arranged neatly in rows and appeared to be made of some sort of red stone, cut in symmetrical shapes. Offshore, tiny fishing boats dotted the surface of the sea. They were all the same size, but of different colors. Treaia was relieved to see that this little town seemed more welcoming than the last village she had been in. Now that she was closer, she could see that the houses were far enough apart for each to have its own garden and small orchard.

Treaia walked uneasily down the main street, which was paved with the same attractive red stone that the houses were made out of. As she was admiring the village, to her surprise a small boy of about ten approached her and said with a smile, "Welcome, my name is Hilo. Have you come a long way?"

Thinking how wonderful it was to be greeted in this friendly fashion, Treaia looked at the boy and began to smile with a warmth that made the boy hold out his hand. "My name is Treaia," she said, taking his hand. "He has the same coloring as Ramana," she thought, "those same green almond-shaped eyes, the dark hair that turns copper in the sun. Could he and Ramana be somehow related?"

Taking Treaia's hand, Hilo started to pull her along, saying, "Come with me to meet my father. He will want to see you."

Walking fast to keep up with him, she saw others moving about, busy with their daily affairs. They did not have the same coloring as Hilo or Ramana. They had fair skin, pale compared with the golden skin of Hilo, and their hair was also light in color. Finally Hilo and Treaia came to a house with a garden in front. Great care had been taken with the arrangement of the flowers. As they walked up the little rock path leading to the front door, the house and garden gave Treaia a warm and friendly feeling. She noticed that white rock had been added around the windows to provide a charming, decorative touch. Hilo hung onto her and threw open the door, shouting, "Father, come and see who I found," as he pulled her into the main room of the house. There in the center of the room was a hearth. It was a nice room, clean and neat, as everything seemed to be in this village.

"You called me, Hilo?" said a man's voice, and a tall, handsome man stood before them with the same eyes and coloring as his son. His hair was graying, and tiny wrinkles crept from the corners of his eyes when he smiled. "Whom have you brought me, my son?" asked the man.

"Her name is Treaia, and she has not been here before," answered Hilo, since that was all he knew.

"How do you do, Treaia. I am Hilo's father, and my name is Lasho. Won't you please sit down and rest from your journey," said the man, offering Treaia a seat with an extended hand.

"Thank you," said Treaia. "I am most grateful for your kindness."

"Before we talk, let us have some refreshment. Hilo, please go to the kitchen and bring the three of us something to drink and eat," commanded Lasho in a gentle tone.

They sat in friendly silence, waiting for Hilo to return, and Treaia felt she had found friends in Hilo and his father. Presently Hilo returned with a tray of food and drink. After serving Treaia, his father, and himself, he sat down and in anticipation of the conversation to come, he asked, "Where did you come from, Treaia? Was it very far from here? Did you have any exciting adventures?"

"Enough, son. Let us not attack her so quickly, with so many questions," Lasho said smiling. "Forgive him, Treaia. He is excited about having a visitor, and like all young boys, yearns to hear of adventure."

"I do not mind. I have questions that I would like to ask you as well," replied Treaia. "Since I am your guest, I will answer you first." She told them all about herself, how she was raised, and the adventures she had had on her way to the village. The more she talked, the wider Hilo's eyes grew. By the time she finished her story, Hilo was leaning almost out of his seat.

"Weren't you awfully frightened?" he asked Treaia. "I would have been too frightened to run away from the evil lord."

"I was terrified many times, Hilo. But we find we do what we have to, in order to survive," Treaia answered, a little surprised to find herself in the role of teacher. "Ramana was the dearest person on this planet to me, and she looked like the two of you, so it makes me feel very happy to see some of her people. Could you please tell me of yourselves and where you came from?"

"I have heard of Ramana, and yes, she was a person like us," Lasho answered. "I will tell you what I know. But first, could you kindly tell me how you were brought to the temple, or from where you were brought?"

"Ramana said that she found me as a small child under strange circumstances and took me for her temple daughter. I was raised, under her care, to become the next high priestess," Treaia answered.

"Then you are the one I heard about," replied Lasho with a warm smile. "I do not remember the land from where I came, since I was very small when my parents arrived here with me. They came from a country on this planet of highly intelligent people. From time to time the leader of this land sends a few of his people to other lands. My parents taught me and raised me here in this village.

"Ramana was taken to the temple when she was young and trained under the high priestess, who was also of our people. Since I was raised in this village, I finally became the leader here. In this way I am able to help the people learn many things. Like the other people of my parents' land, I have the ability to see visions, which help me to teach the people and my son Hilo, who will guide them after me. My parents knew of Ramana and her purpose, which was to raise you."

On hearing Lasho's words, Treaia sat for a long time lost in thought, and finally tears started running down her cheeks. "I have failed Ramana so miserably," she cried. "All I cared about was myself. Each time I had a choice I thought only of myself and my own desires, and I didn't even remember the things Ramana taught me until my life was endangered."

Lasho came over to Treaia and put his fatherly arms around her. "Dear child," he said, "it is not how often we fall down, but how we pick ourselves up that counts." Waiting until a smile again came to Treaia's lips, he asked, "Now if you will, please tell us of your plan."

"When I knew I was safe from Tartek," said Treaia, feeling reassured, "I slept and had a dream. In the dream I was told to come here and wait for one with a sword who would come for me."

"Ah, you have visions also," said Lasho. "You shall stay with us until your dream is fulfilled. We will be happy with your company. Although we try to teach all we know to the people here, they do not accept much. They are slow in learning. So it will be good to have someone to talk to, someone who has also learned some of the lessons of life."

"I would like that, thank you. Perhaps you can help me learn how to use some of the things Ramana taught me," Treaia said.

Treaia was happy living with Lasho and Hilo; they were like the father and brother she had never had. She spent part of her days in helping to care for the house and gardens. Sometimes she would go and talk to the townspeople and take long walks on the beach. Most of all she enjoyed talking with Lasho.

One day while sitting in the garden, Treaia asked Lasho, "Yours is the only house that is any different from the others, yet the tiny fishing boats are of varied colors. Can you explain why?"

"Let me ask you a question before I answer," Lasho said. "You have talked to many of the people here. What can you tell me about them?"

"Let me think," said Treaia, puckering her forehead in concentration. "They all have basically the same thoughts and talk of the same things—their gardens, houses, and boats. They have no interest in being different from one another. I see now—that is why their houses are alike. The people are so much alike that they think alike."

"Yes, Treaia, what you noticed was no individuality," said Lasho, pointing to the houses up the street. "Individuality is a step upward in evolution, when a person does not have to think the thoughts of his neighbor or live just like his neighbor. I feel I can be a little different because I am their leader, but I am careful not to be too different. Too much difference between neighbors, in these people, brings about fear, and fear we do not need, since it is the cause of hatred. You had that experience in the primitive village, where you were almost sacrificed because you were different."

"I remember too well, Lasho," said Treaia, thinking again of the knife that the old chieftain had almost thrust into her heart. "But what of the boats. Why does each have its own separate color?"

"The boats are a small step in the direction of individuality. I suggested to the townspeople that if each fisherman had a boat of a different color, when the wives looked out they would be able to tell which boat belonged to their husband or son. They liked this idea, so each chose a different color from his neighbor. This made them think and be different, although only for the short time it took to color their boats. But a step at a time is the only way we all can progress, and one step after another leads us to where we are going in the end."

As Treaia was walking down the beach one clear afternoon when not even a small cloud was to be seen, she was thinking how happy she had been here with Hilo and Lasho. It was the first happiness she had had since Ramana had been killed. She thought back to the day she had been on the beach when the temple had been destroyed and Ramana had given her the jewels, telling her to find the missing part. "I will find the missing part, Ramana," she said to the sea as the tide rushed in.

Listening to the surf while the warm sun bathed her body made Treaia sleepy, so she sat down on the sand and let it gently drift through her fingers as she admired the blue-green of the water. Drowsily thinking of what lay on the other side of this large span of water, she fell asleep, curled up on the sparkling white sand.

Not too far away, a young prince was riding toward the sea. When Mey had left Tartek's forest, he had not known at first which way to go, until a beautiful bird, all white except for a black head, had appeared in the sky above him and headed south. The bird had seemed like a sign to Mey, so he had decided to follow its direction. The bird was always there, leading the way. Even when he had slept at night, the next day the bird would circle above him and continue. Now, after several days, Mey finally reached the sea and a long, sandy white beach. Still following the bird, but thinking that perhaps he was foolish to do so, Mey made his way along the beach. "I must find food soon," he said to himself. "I've eaten nothing since escaping from Tartek's forest. I'll follow the shoreline for a while and perhaps I'll meet someone. If not, I'll have to turn around and go another way."

As he rode down the beach, Mey said to Kala in a

tired voice, "I no longer see the bird, so maybe it is time to turn around and head another way. But look, Kala! There is someone up ahead, lying on the sand." Excited to see a human being again after such a long time, Mey dismounted and walked up to the sleeping figure. "Hello there," he said, addressing the figure, which seemed to be that of a young girl.

Sleep still in her eyes, Treaia raised herself to a sitting position as she heard the voice call out to her. Turning to see where this strangely familiar voice came from, she saw Mey looking down on her. "Who are you?" she asked in surprise.

Mey walked closer. "Could you tell me . . ." he began to say, but he did not finish speaking. On seeing her face he could only stare; and then his head started to spin and he fainted from hunger.

Treaia jumped up in alarm as the young man fell to the sand. She ran over to see if she could help, but he lay there very still. His horse was licking his head, as if trying to help. Then Kala moved over closer to Treaia and nudged her. "If you will hold still, my friend," she said to the horse, "maybe I can get him on your back and we can take him home for help." After a struggle she succeeded in getting Mey onto the horse's back.

"Who do you have there?" Lasho called as Treaia made her way down the path to the house.

"I was taking a nap on the beach when this young man rode up on his horse. He was about to tell me his name but he fainted. I don't know what could be the matter with him," answered Treaia in an anxious voice.

Lasho quickly lifted Mey from the horse, took him into the house, and laid him down. He sent Treaia to the kitchen for water.

"He seems awfully thin," said Lasho. "He doesn't seem to have been eating well. And look how tattered his clothes are. I think he's in some sort of delirium. For now the important thing is to try to get a little soup and light food into him." Hilo took care of Kala and gave him a warm place to spend the night.

Several hours later, Lasho, Treaia, and Hilo saw their visitor's eyes finally begin to flutter.

"Where am I? Who are you?" Mey whispered. Seeing Lasho, he tried to get up.

"It's all right, my son; don't get up yet. You became sick from hunger and from too much traveling. Don't talk yet, go back to sleep and we can talk tomorrow," Lasho told him kindly.

This reassured Mey and he quickly closed his eyes and went back to sleep—this time a sound sleep, without the delirium.

"I think he will be fine now, just as soon as he has a little more rest. Let's go outside and talk, so as not to disturb him," Lasho said, taking Treaia's and Hilo's arms and guiding them out of the room.

When they were outside Treaia said with a puzzled look on her face, "Did you hear him muttering my name? And did you hear him mention a sword and that he reached the temple too late, only to find it destroyed?"

"Yes, I heard the same things as you did. It seems that he may be the one you were waiting for, doesn't it?" smiled Lasho.

"I don't know how he knew my name. He might have a sword, but I'm sure he couldn't be the one I have dreamed of," Treaia said with indignation.

"Why are you so sure?" questioned Lasho.

"Well, for one thing, he is young, not mature like the man I dreamed of. He seems very nice," she said thoughtfully, "but he doesn't seem to shine and sparkle like I remember." Treaia frowned and wrinkled up her nose in a puzzled fashion.

"Remember that you are also young, my dear. Now, I think we should all go to bed so that we might be fresh when he awakes. Good night," Lasho said, as he walked toward his room.

"Good morning," Lasho said as he smiled down at Treaia the next day. "Hilo and the young man, whose name is Mey, went for a short walk in the garden. We were up hours before you this day. Didn't you sleep well?"

"I tossed and turned all night. For some reason I felt restless," Treaia yawned.

"Sit down and have some breakfast, while I tell you Mey's story," Lasho said. He told Treaia the whole story, and when he reached the end, Mey and Hilo returned to the house.

"I am indeed grateful to you and in your debt for helping me yesterday," Mey said, as he sat down at the table opposite Treaia, thinking to himself how young and lovely she was. "But how could she be the high priestess or the girl in my dreams?" he thought. "She seems so young, and I am surely searching after knowledge and wisdom."

"I am glad Lasho has told you my story," he said. "Did he also tell you about the sword, and that I am seeking the keeper of the jewels?"

Treaia remembered that the voice had told her to wait for the one with the sword. She felt a strange warmth growing in her toward this young man, but there was another feeling of hesitation that fought against it. He was not as she had imagined, in so many ways. "Which feeling should I listen to?" thought Treaia, as she asked Mey, "You talked of a powerful sword. May we see it?"

"Indeed, yes," said Mey, who, like Treaia, was conscious of conflicting feelings in his own heart. He took the sword out of the box and placed it carefully on the table.

"It is beautiful," the others said in amazement, as they looked at its shining splendor.

Treaia untied the bag she kept at her waist, and poured the jewels out for everyone to see. She looked long and deeply at Mey, feeling the affection within her begin to grow. "This sword must be the other half I was sent to find," she said, as she patiently set the stones into their proper places, until every shining stone had a bed in which to rest.

The magnificence of the sword and the stones took everyone's breath away. "Who could have imagined that each would enhance the other so," said Mey in awe. "Both were beautiful before, but together they have a new strength."

After a time Lasho asked, "What is the secret now that the two of you have the whole of it together?"

"I do not know," Mey said, as he looked toward Treaia. "Do you?" he asked her.

"No," said Treaia softly, "I don't. I can only think that perhaps the sword and the stones have come together to show us something about ourselves." Mey took her hand and smiled, filled with the sensation that his search would no longer be lonely, and Treaia smiled in return. "Perhaps the mature man of knowledge of my dreams *will* appear in my life," she thought, looking into Mey's eyes and far into the future.

Chapter Eleven

Three In A Boat

As Mey was regaining his health, the days settled into a pleasant routine. He spent many of his days with Lasho and Hilo, working on their latest project, a new kind of boat. It was a much larger boat than was generally used or needed in the village, but Lasho still did not know why he was building it. He had had a vision in which he had seen himself building a boat to certain specifications, and he always followed his visions, even though sometimes he did not find out the purpose until later. After dinner the four of them would sit around talking. There was always something interesting to learn when talking with Lasho.

Treaia began to think of Mey as her friend. She had always wanted a friend. She began to realize that friends didn't have to be perfect, but that people had to have other people to share things with—their hopes and their failures. It began to feel good to her to have someone to talk with who had gone through some of the same experiences as she.

One evening, while they were sitting and talking to Lasho, Treaia remarked, "You know, my friends, talking and listening to Mey have made me see more clearly the imperfections in my own character. I can see how self-centered I have been, amongst other things. I know I failed from time to time, yet I never really changed because of that, nor do I know if I will ever overcome these faults of mine. Can you tell me what I should do?"

Before Lasho could answer, Mey said in a subdued tone, "She is explaining exactly what I have been feeling too."

Lasho smiled kindly at them and said, "The most important thing toward your advancement you have both done: you have begun to realize your imperfections of character. Until now you saw them, but only intellectually, and people must understand themselves in their *hearts* before they can really change anything. Have you decided what you are going to do?" he added.

"I was sent to search for knowledge and the secret of the sword, to bring them home to my people," said Mey thoughtfully. "Although I have learned much from observing your leadership and listening to your wisdom, from meeting Treaia, and from the sword and the stones,

I am still not sure if I have found the secret. I feel that the best thing would be to go home again to my kingdom with Treaia, and continue to search for the secret there. Do you agree?"

"I am sure you both will find the secret," said Lasho. "The important thing is that you found each other, even though you still don't understand all the reasons for that. You are both very young and have yet to go through much preparation. I think it would be a good idea to return to your kingdom to try to find out more clearly the needs of your people."

"Will you go too, Treaia?" asked Hilo.

"I have been very happy here," said Treaia. "It's been wonderful to have a family. But I feel a strange need to keep searching, for the secret also, perhaps. Would you like me to come with you, Mey?" she asked.

"I would be most grateful for your company, Treaia. Please come with me. There will always be a home and place for you at the palace in my kingdom," Mey said.

"If you will allow me to advise you, Treaia," Lasho said. "Let me say that I myself have always followed my visions and my intuitions, and they have all turned out to have been the right thing to do. Sometimes dreams fade, or we change them ourselves after time has passed. Do not hold on to an old dream; allow yourself to follow the promptings of your inner voice."

"In that case," Treaia said with a smile, "I must go with you, Mey, and we will find our fortune together. But," and a cloud crossed her face as she remembered, "I do not want to go back through Tartek's forest."

"Let us see if we can work out another route," said Lasho. "There is usually more than one way to get anywhere." He brought a pen and paper and began to draw. "This is the shape of our continent, and this is where we are now. Help me fill in where you have been."

Treaia marked the way back to the lake and through the forest of deception and the village of the primitives to the temple. Then Mey worked his way back over the mountains, through the barren land to his kingdom. He drew in his kingdom as best he could, showing where the sea was and where the mountains were. As they all looked at the map they had made, they could see that parts were unknown to them. But they could also see that if they followed the coast around, eventually they would come to Mey's kingdom.

"Now I know at last why I built the boat!" Lasho exclaimed happily. "It was for you, so that you might return home."

"How exciting this is!" Treaia said joyfully. "I have never been in a boat before."

Once the decision was made, everyone became excited and busy making preparations. They spent several days putting the finishing touches to the boat and gathering supplies. Lasho also helped Mey make a scabbard so that he could carry his sword by his side.

Lasho and Hilo were up before dawn on the day of the trip. "Why do you look so sad, Hilo?" asked Lasho, seeing the boy hang his head forlornly.

"Why is it that we cannot go on trips, see the world, and have adventures like Mey and Treaia?" asked Hilo.

"I asked that very same question of my mother and father when I was about your age," said Lasho. "I will tell you the same thing that I was told, and you will be given the same choice that I was given." Lasho took the boy by the arm and led him to the bow of the boat, so that they could look over the sea and watch the light play on the water as the sun came up.

Putting his arm around Hilo's shoulder he began, "We have been given the ability of seeing true visions that help us do our work, and if we did not do the task set out for us, we would soon lose this ability. It is lonely at times for us, but to be of true service to our world is the only way we or anyone can grow into something better. We descend from a very intelligent race of people. I do not know where on this continent they exist, but exist they do. My parents lived there until it was time for them to come here and do their job.

"Also, Hilo, you should know that it is possible for people to travel in other ways than by boat. If people concentrate and practice patiently, they can learn how to leave their bodies when they are sleeping at night, or when they are lying out under a tree somewhere, dreaming of another place. I have done this myself, so I know for sure that the land of our forefathers does exist on this continent. Concentrate on Mey and Treaia, and you will be able to visit them for a short while after they are gone.

"You, my son, could leave this place when you are grown, for no one would stop you, not even I. But if you decide to leave, know that it may be many lives before you again have this opportunity to serve. You chose to be born for this service. As you grow, you will be given visions to show that what I speak to you is the truth."

"Thank you for telling me, father. I feel better now about having to stay in our village," said Hilo as he hugged his father. "Now I have something to do for Treaia before we go join them for breakfast."

Their last meal together had an undertone of melancholia. Hilo smiled at Treaia and said, "I shall miss you very much. But father has told me that I can learn to travel without my body. I will practice and come and visit you wherever you are. Do you know how to travel this way?"

Walking over to Hilo and kneeling down to look at him face-to-face, Treaia said affectionately, "Hilo, you are like a brother to me." She took his face in her hands and kissed him on both cheeks. "I love you dearly, and I shall miss you very much. Yes, I have done some of this kind of traveling you are speaking of. But I am not as good at it as I shall be when I'm a little older, since, like you, I need to practice. I promise I will practice very hard. You do the same thing, and we will visit each other whenever we like. You will always have a special place in my heart."

"Wait until you see the surprise I have for you," Hilo said as they headed for the boat.

When Treaia and Mey saw the boat, they both hugged Hilo in delight at what he had done. The boat was decorated all over with flowers, even on top of the mast.

As Hilo was hugging Treaia goodbye, he whispered in her ear so that no one else could hear, "Just in case you get married one day, these flowers are for your wedding. I will not be able to be there." Treaia kissed him.

"Just follow the coastline and you will reach your kingdom," said Lasho. "We will miss you, but we know your destiny lies elsewhere."

With that, they warmly embraced once more, and Mey and Treaia climbed aboard. They asked Kala to lie down, to ensure that he would not fall out if the boat tipped. They had agreed beforehand that Kala was to go, since there had been no truer friend than he, and he deserved to return to his home. Waving goodbye and trying to smile through the tears that welled up in his eyes—for it was hard to leave these dear friends—Mey pushed the boat adrift.

They watched and waved to Hilo and Lasho until they rounded the bend and the village was no longer in view. Soon all they could see, landward, were gigantic cliffs, and green water with caps of white, moving in to land, was their view in the opposite direction. Kala lay still in the boat and seemed to understand what was happening. His trust in Mey was sure enough not to let this strange experience trouble him needlessly. There was a sail on the boat, and at the stern a long paddlelike oar to use as a rudder, to keep the boat going in the right direction. They sailed on swiftly with the currents.

There was excitement in the air. Mey and Treaia were young and the thrill of the journey soon raced through their blood.

"It's much more fun to have company on a journey," Mey said, smiling at Treaia. "I'm glad you came."

"So am I," and she smiled back.

Smelling the sea air and pleased with the fragrance of the flowers, Treaia remembered what Hilo had whispered to her. Turning to Mey where he stood guiding the boat, she said, "I once dreamed of a building that had a different shape from any I have ever seen. It was triangular. Are there buildings like that in your kingdom?"

"I had a dream about a similar building; isn't that strange?" said Mey. "But no, there is no structure like that where I come from. If we both dreamed about one, where do you suppose the building is, if it exists? I wish we had thought to ask Lasho," Mey added.

"There seem to be so many things we have learned, and yet so much we do not understand. Even so, everything seems so wonderful, so vital and exciting, like this sea we are riding on." Treaia spoke with eyes dancing, full of life.

But suddenly the boat began shaking and they heard a loud rumbling.

"What's that?" called Mey in alarm, stumbling as the boat rocked.

Looking all around her, Treaia pointed up to the cliffs. "See, up there, at the top of the cliffs, I think it's a volcano," she called out. "I have never seen one, but I have heard people talk about them." Following Treaia's pointing finger, Mey could see a huge cone-shaped mountain top, out of which smoke was pouring at a rapid rate. "I was told that sometimes the crust of the land opens up, and through this opening comes lava or melted rocks," explained Treaia.

"You will have to teach me about volcanoes," Mey said, and in the next breath grabbed hold of her. The boat shook so fiercely that he thought she might fall over.

Laughing as he grabbed her, Treaia said, "Look, Mey, the lava is starting to come out of the top of the volcano. It looks like liquid fire running down the sides. Isn't it beautiful to see, this work of nature!"

They did not recognize the danger they were in as they watched the inferno becoming more and more violent. But soon the water was churning so roughly that Mey could hardly hold on to the rudder. The lava was rolling so fast now that it was coming into the sea. It was so hot and moving with such momentum that the water did not put out the fire. Treaia helped Mey hang on to the rudder, but the currents kept pulling them into the fiery path. There was fire on both sides of them now, and a thick steam arose where the fire met the water. Both Mey and Treaia struggled to keep the boat on a middle course between two tongues of fire, since they realized that if they got too close to either side, the fire would destroy them and the boat. The sea no longer looked so beautiful. Perspiration ran down their faces from the intense heat. Both were secretly thinking that this was perhaps the end. Looking down at Kala to see if he was all right, Mey noticed that Kala acted as if he were asleep. He was not excited at all.

"Hang on to me tightly, Treaia," screamed Mey over the pounding, rumbling noise of the eruption and the sizzling sound of the fire entering the water.

Treaia held on to Mey tightly. If she had not, she would have been thrown in all directions, since the boat was now tumbling from side to side, from bow to stern. "Just keep us between the fire and we'll make it," yelled Treaia. The noise was so loud and deafening that they could not hear one another very well. They clung to each other more tightly and held the rudder as steady as they could. It was hard to see where they were because of the steam.

All of a sudden there was silence. A dead stillness fell upon them, and it felt as though the boat were floating down a smooth path. The fog lifted and the fire stood on both sides of them like walls. There was not one bit of damage to the boat, nor was one flower destroyed.

"Are we dreaming, Mey?" whispered Treaia, still shaking.

"I don't know," answered Mey, looking pale and ashen.

Out of nowhere a rumbling voice spoke to them. "Just as you are guiding your craft through the fire upon the water, so must you guide yourselves through life, without being consumed by zeal or destroyed by truth." It was a deep voice that gave the impression of surrounding them completely.

"Did you hear that?" Mey asked Treaia, open-mouthed. Treaia nodded, and the voice began to speak again.

"My domain, the water, is the medium from which all form sprang on this planet. The great lives of our system use water to symbolize life itself, which is not the form. There is another use for water in both the form sense and the symbolic sense, and that is cleansing. The waters wash away the mud and slime of nature's growth."

Then there was stillness again, except for the breathing of the three in the boat, until unexpectedly a wall of fire loomed ahead of them, and spread all around the boat. Mey held on tightly to Treaia. Both closed their eyes, knowing there was no turning back, while flames danced on all sides and the boat was completely engulfed with fire. Opening her eyes, Treaia said, "I don't understand, Mey, we are surrounded by fire, and yet I feel no heat or burning on my body. Are we really here?"

"We're still alive; that's all that matters," replied Mey. "Listen, do you hear a voice again?"

As they listened, a high-pitched voice, dancing rhythmically, seemed to come from the center of their heads. "Fire always carries forward that which water has begun," spoke the voice. "When the fire of purification met the water of life, vapor rose, as the spirit rises to attain new heights of pure living. Fire is the burning of lessons in life that clears away the obstacles to growth. Fire releases all that blocks the way of life. Fire destroys the veils. Fire takes many forms. Fire is the symbol of intellect."

As the last note of the voice sounded, they noticed that the fire was now behind them. The sun shone, and the water was blue and clear; a soft breeze pushed them on their way. Overcome by their ordeal, Mey and Treaia stood in silence. Then a gentle whispering seemed to pass through them, and another voice murmured, "Air is the carrier of all energies, such as the divine force of life and the spirit through which that life must manifest itself. Air is the symbol of spiritual love—a symbol of a higher life, which gives freedom of experience, where the soul comes into full expression. One more thing I leave with you. When water, land, and air meet, there you will find the greatest magic."

Then everything around them returned to normal, and they could hear the sounds of the sea again. Mey and Treaia found they were able to speak once more, but they felt paralyzed by the astounding events they had just been through.

"What was that? Whose were the voices that spoke to us?" Treaia asked Mey anxiously.

"I don't understand what happened, but perhaps we will one day. The voices reminded me of the wise one of the land," answered Mey in a reverent tone.

"Whatever their reason for appearing to us, I am sure that the three voices must have been the wise ones of water, fire, and air. But I didn't understand one thing that was said. How can people be destroyed by truth? Did you understand that, Treaia?" asked Mey.

"I think perhaps the wise one meant that if you are false, truth will destroy you," Treaia answered. "I was taught this by Ramana, and I learned my lesson well in Tartek's land."

A whinny came from Kala. Now he was awake, after sleeping through the whole ordeal. He seemed restless, and wanted to get up. He had not been able to stretch his long legs for many hours.

"There's a nice beach over there. Let's land for a while and give poor Kala a rest, and it will be nice for us too," said Mey.

"Yes, let's, it looks like a lovely place for our meal. All of a sudden I'm very hungry," Treaia said in agreement.

Mey jumped out of the boat, pulled it up on the sand, and moored it as best he could. Kala pranced with enjoyment at being back on his legs.

"No wonder we were so hungry, it's starting to get dark. I didn't realize that we had been gone the whole day," said Treaia in surprise.

"Dawn to dusk and yet it seems like a short time to have gone through so much. Let's camp here on this nice beach for the night, and get an early start again tomorrow," said Mey, as Kala neighed his approval.

Mey and Treaia fell asleep watching the stars and thinking of the strange, exciting boat trip they had had that day.

Chapter Twelve

The City

"What a marvelous morning this is," Treaia said, as she woke up feeling light and airy. Looking around her at the lovely beach and the high sheer cliffs, she pirouetted happily. "Mey, do you feel like this? I feel new, somehow reborn, as though a great weight has been lifted off me."

"Yes, I feel the same way," said Mey.

"It feels almost as if I had awoken to a new world," Treaia said, looking toward the boat, or to where the boat should have been. "But it's gone!" she called out in disbelief. "Our boat is gone!"

Both ran to the water's edge to see if they could locate the missing boat, but it was nowhere in sight. It seemed to have disappeared completely.

"I don't understand this at all. I know I moored the boat well, so the tide could not have taken it out," said Mey miserably.

Treaia put her hands on Mey's shoulders to comfort him. "Please let's not panic yet," she said. "Let's have some breakfast, then we can decide what to do."

Spreading a cloth on the sand, Treaia unpacked their food and water from the baskets they had unloaded from the boat. They ate silently, depressed about their unhappy situation. When they finished eating, Treaia suggested, "Perhaps we should explore a bit; we might find something that will help us." The idea of exploring brought a smile to her face.

"Excellent idea," said Mey as he got up; he liked exploring as much as Treaia.

But they found nothing new, only the cliff of sand, so steep and so sheer that they could not even find a fingerhold to begin scaling it. Also, the cliff was so high they could not tell what kind of terrain was on top. Disappointed, they returned to their camp and sat down on the sand.

"Well, what now?" Treaia said thoughtfully, as they both looked out to sea, scanning the horizon for their boat.

"We're stranded on a desolate beach; soon there will be no food or water. Is this what we've come to?" Mey said as he dismally threw a pebble into the sea.

Unable to think of a way out, both sat and watched the breakers in deep thought, when to their astonishment they suddenly heard a sound. "Welcome," said a deep voice. They jumped up and saw a man and a woman standing behind them, dressed in white tunics of the finest linen. A purple cord was tied to the waist of each. Their hair glistened copper in the sun, and their almond-green eyes immediately caught Treaia's attention. The woman spoke. "We were told to expect you. You are Mey and Treaia?"

Surprised to see anyone, let alone people who looked like Ramana, Lasho, and Hilo, Mey and Treaia nodded in response to the question. Seeing the surprise on their faces, the man stepped forward and held out his hand in a friendly fashion, saying, "I am Nebo, and this is my wife, Tura."

"We didn't realize you didn't know you were expected," Tura said and smiled.

"I am sorry we were so startled; this is a lovely surprise. We are indeed happy to meet you," said Treaia as she held out her hands to both of them, Mey joining in.

"We have just left some of your people before coming here—Lasho and his young son, Hilo," said Mey, pleased.

"Yes, we have heard of them, although we have not met them in person," said Nebo. "Now if you will come with us, we will escort you to our city."

They followed Tura and Nebo, who led the way to the smooth wall of stone that arose above them. Still not knowing how they were to get off the beach, but keeping these thoughts to themselves, Mey's and Treaia's eyes opened wide as Nebo pushed on the wall and a door slid open, revealing a small room within. "If you will step inside, please, this will take us to our destination," motioned Tura.

"What about Kala, my horse?" asked Mey.

"I know how it can be accomplished," Tura said to Nebo. "We will use the pulley and ropes."

"Come now, and we will bring your horse presently," said Nebo, as he ushered them into the small room.

Trustingly Treaia and Mey stepped inside the room, along with Nebo and Tura. The stone door closed, but it was not dark. Some form of light glowed inside. They began to feel a moving sensation and Treaia said, "My stomach feels very upset. Why should that be? And how are we to get up the cliff by standing in this small room?"

"I have the same sensation of movement," added Mey.

"Again we are sorry, we should have known that you have never ridden in a lift before," Nebo said smiling, thinking of what they must be feeling. "This little room moves up and down on a large cable. There is a door that opens onto the beach, and one that opens at the top, where our city is. We will show you how it is operated when we finish the ascent."

Just as Nebo finished speaking, they came to a stop and the door opened again. Stepping out, Mey and Treaia could scarcely believe their eyes. Rich green lawn met their feet like a living carpet, thick and luxurious, and palm trees of every size were in view, with flowering bushes scattered about. There were no buildings to be seen, although they looked for the city.

"The city is over the knoll," Tura said. "But first we will get your horse."

Nebo took a very long, heavy rope from a small room by the lift. He tied it to a machine in the same room, then turning to Mey he said, "You go back down in the lift with Tura, and when the rope is let down over the cliff, securely tie it around your horse. Pull the rope three times when ready. After you see that he is safely up, come back up in the lift." Mey went back down with Tura. Nebo dropped the rope over the edge, and turning to Treaia, he asked her, "Please hold loosely to the rope and when you feel the tug three times, motion to me and I will start the machinery."

Treaia stood with the rope in her hands, waiting. Finally she felt the tugs and waved to Nebo, who activated the machinery and the rope started to come up. Soon she heard Kala making frightened, whimpering noises, and eventually he came into sight. Treaia ran up to Kala and hugged him. "Dear Kala, that must have been an awful ride for you. But it was the only way for you to come with us. We wouldn't want to be without you," she told him affectionately.

"I will engage the lift and Mey and Tura will be back up soon," Nebo called from the little room, where he was pushing and pulling levers and buttons.

Soon the door to the lift opened and out stepped Tura and Mey. Mey gave Treaia's hand a squeeze, and said, "Isn't it wonderful what these two have accomplished, bringing Kala up a sheer cliff like that? Tura made a girdle for Kala to wear, so the rope would not hurt him." Mey took the rope and girdle off Kala, and the three walked over to the small room where Nebo and Tura were putting things back in order.

"What force do you use to make the cable go up and down?" asked Mey, excited at what he had seen.

"We use the energy from the sun. The sun's rays are captured in many crystals. Later I'll show you the arrangement of the crystals just outside the city," answered Nebo.

"If we are all ready, we should go now. It's about dinner time and I'm hungry," said Tura.

On reaching the top of the knoll, they had a marvelous view of the city. Mey and Treaia came to an abrupt halt, spellbound with its beauty. Most of the buildings had tall fluted columns in front, with many steps leading up to the entrances. Canals ran throughout the city, with large, grand fountains in the parklike areas in front of the buildings. Mey turned to Treaia enthusiastically. "I've seen many places on this continent but this is like stepping into another world!" he exclaimed.

Seeing the pleased look which their city brought to the faces of their guests, Tura said with pride, "There is no other city on this planet like the city of Nerius."

Pointing to the right, amazed at what he saw, Mey asked, "What is that dome-shaped building with the revolving roof?"

"That is one of the ways we study the heavens," answered Nebo.

"Oh, Mey, look over to your left. See that triangle-shaped building. It's like the one we dreamed of," said Treaia, as she took in a deep breath of exhilaration.

"But in my dream it did not seem so gigantic, or so beautiful," gasped Mey in admiration.

Mey and Treaia could not take their eyes off this building, which sloped from its huge base upward, toward a high sharp peak, truncating near the top to provide a platform. They could see that one of the sides was smooth but the other had stairs in the middle, leading to the top.

"What is it made of? It looks white and glistens with gold sparkles," asked Treaia.

"That building is faced with gold quartz. We have an abundance of this quartz and use it for decoration here in Nerius," explained Nebo.

"But we will answer all your questions later. First let us go and rest," said Tura.

For the rest of the way into the city, Mey and Treaia walked in silent wonder and admiration at all the beautiful and mysterious things they saw. Coming to the steps of one of the buildings with the columns, Nebo called a man over and asked him to tend to Kala. Smiling as if pleased to assist, the man took Kala with him.

"I noticed that everyone wears the same type of tunic, but some have different colored cords about their waists. Can you tell us why?" asked Mey.

"Since we all dress similarly, the color of the cords tells which station in life we hold. See that man coming down the stairs wearing the brown cord? He is a doctor of medicine," Tura said, as they made their way up the stairs and into the building.

"We will take you to your rooms, so that you may freshen up. There are clean tunics for you. We will call for you in a few moments," Nebo said, as he led each one to their own room.

Entering her room, Treaia found the marble floor was smooth and cool to her touch. The room had a rare beauty and simplicity of design, and she walked over to look out of the large window casements. She now understood why the buildings had to be reached by so many steps. From this height everyone had a view of the sea. Seeing that there was a room adjoining, she entered, and found a large sunken oval pool, full of warm scented water, and the clean tunic that had been promised her laid out on a marble bench. After disrobing, Treaia bathed in the pool and clothed herself in the fresh white tunic. There was a golden cord to tie around her waist. She had just finished brushing her long, rich, black hair, when a knock came on the door. Treaia hurried to answer.

Standing there were Tura, Nebo, and Mey. "Are you ready to join us for dinner?" smiled Tura.

"Indeed I am. Thank you for the lovely room and this tunic," Treaia said, as she walked with them to the dining room, which was a large oval room with cathedral windows on three sides. The tables were set with places for four, and all places were filled except at the table to which Nebo led them. Perhaps fifty people were dining in the room. All looked similar in coloring and clothes, except for their different colored cords. Halfway through dinner, which consisted of many varieties of fruit, vegetables, and breads, Nebo rose. All was suddenly silent until he spoke. "I would like to introduce you to our guests, Mey and Treaia. Please make them welcome to all of our activities."

Mey and Treaia stood, acknowledging the welcome and thanking their new hosts. After dinner they were led back to their rooms, and told that the next day they would be shown many things of interest.

Treaia was barely inside her door when she heard a soft knocking. Opening the door, she saw Mey standing there. "Would you like to walk for a while before going to sleep?" he asked her.

"That would be lovely; I am too excited to sleep," answered Treaia as she stepped out of her room.

They walked down the long, wide flight of stairs and over to one of the fountains, where the water was spraying up and down in many colors.

"Isn't it beautiful here? And all the people are like Ramana and Lasho. What a wonderful place to live! Did you notice at dinner that no other wore a gold colored cord, except you and me? Maybe gold means guests," Treaia said, answering her own question. "What's more, no one but you was wearing a sword, but no one seemed to notice your sword. It's strange."

"Many things are strange. We were expected, but how did they know we were coming here, when even we didn't know? Every time I tried to ask, they avoided answering, yet in such a manner that I forgot I had asked the question until now. What do you think of it?" Mey said, with a perplexed look on his face.

"You are right about their knowing we were coming.

They even had clothes ready for us. The only answer I can think of is Lasho. Lasho must have contacted them," Treaia answered, as puzzled as Mey.

"Yes, maybe Lasho told them about us. He is very wise, and knows many more things than he told us, I'm sure," said Mey.

"But it doesn't really matter," said Treaia. "Even with all our questions, I think being here in Nerius is the most wonderful thing that has ever happened to me."

"Treaia, look to your left," Mey said, sucking his breath in sharply. A large disc, shining brightly, was hovering over the city. Then it turned and disappeared behind the round building with the moving dome.

"I've never seen anything like that before, not even in my dreams," exclaimed Treaia. "There seem to be so many things for us to learn here; I am anxious for tomorrow. Let's retire for the night so we will be rested when Nebo and Tura come for us."

Mey and Treaia said goodnight happily; it had indeed been a very exciting day.

Tura came for Mey and Treaia early in the morning, and they met Nebo in the dining room, where the four breakfasted together.

"Last night Treaia and I saw a brilliant disc hover over the city. Can you please tell us what it was?" Mey asked.

"You saw one of our aircraft. Eventually you will be shown one, in the process of seeing and learning about our city. Everyone who visits our land is given an opportunity to learn what we know and our methods. Since you are here, we hope you will stay for a time and learn many things," said Nebo.

"Thank you. I believe I am truly ready to learn now. To be given this chance is more than I could have asked for. If I can learn the knowledge that is here in Nerius I will really be able to help my own people." Then, turning to Treaia, he thought, "I hope she wants to stay too. I'm beginning to be very used to Treaia. She has become a real friend to me."

"I wish to stay too. I already love it here," Treaia said, her eyes sparkling. "I hope I can stay here always," she thought to herself.

"We will start your tour in the library," Nebo said, as he led them out of the room.

"Are you the ruler of Nerius?" asked Treaia as they walked along.

"No, King Nerius rules this land. We are his workers," answered Tura. "When the time is right, you shall have the privilege of meeting him."

The four of them went up the stairs to an even larger building than the one they had just left, inside of which was a room with a ceiling higher than they had ever seen. On three walls were books, from floor to ceiling. In the center of the room were tables with many different objects on them, including glass tubes and a burner with a fire. On the fourth wall, in front of the windows, was a podium, behind which stood a man with soft gray hair and many wrinkles at the corners of his green eyes. He was talking to about fifteen men and women with purple cords tied to their white tunics, sitting in a semicircle around the podium. On seeing them enter, the gray-haired man stopped speaking and waited for their approach. "This is Doctor Zar. He will be your head instructor. Only King Nerius knows more than he," Nebo said, as he introduced Mey and Treaia.

"Welcome to Nerius," said Doctor Zar. "As soon as I excuse my class I will accompany you on your tour."

"We will show you a glimpse of the stars," said Doctor Zar, and they went into the building with the moving roof.

"How can we see the stars during the day, inside a building?" asked Mey.

"You will see shortly," answered Tura, and they moved to the center of the room where a large round object stood, extending up to the round domed ceiling.

"Make yourselves comfortable," Doctor Zar said, motioning to places for them to sit.

Doctor Zar moved different pieces of equipment first one way, then another. It became very dark. The large round object moved slowly and its center opened wide. There were the stars! As it moved, they could see a panorama of the heavens before them—more stars than they had ever seen. Doctor Zar named each large mass of stars as it moved into view.

"This is surely a dream come true," said Mey in fascination.

Doctor Zar moved the equipment again. Soon everything was the same as before, with light again coming into the room. "You will start learning the ways of the stars tomorrow, in one of your classes," Doctor Zar said, leading the small group outside.

The day was spent going from building to building, but never once did they go close to the great building shaped like a triangle. Exclaiming over the many wonderful sights of the day, Mey and Treaia could not thank their hosts enough during dinner for sharing their city with them.

"I have watched the stars all my life, but I never saw them as we did today," said Mey.

Treaia nodded in agreement.

"We still have time before retiring to take you to see the stars through a different medium," said Nebo happily. He was enjoying showing Mey and Treaia all of Nerius.

After walking for some distance, they came to the colossal sloping structure faced with gold quartz that Mey and Treaia were so fascinated with.

"What do you call this beautiful structure?" asked Treaia.

"We just call it the tower," answered Tura.

"Are we going inside?" Treaia asked hopefully.

"No, we will climb the stairs to the top. I have never been inside. Nor has anyone I know of, since there is no door. We use it as an observation point and a place to look at the stars at night," said Nebo, leading the way to the stairs.

"How was this fabulous tower built?" asked Mey.

"It was built a long time ago, way before our time, and I was told by Doctor Zar that the massive cut stones were put in place by some kind of chanting. If you want to know more, you will have to talk to Doctor Zar or King Nerius," said Nebo.

Even with the smooth steps it was a long climb to the platform at the top, which was recessed, forming a wall about chest height. It was a very large area, and the view of the city was spectacular. On the wall was a stand of some sort that held a long black object. "Look into the small end," Nebo suggested to Mey.

"Magnificent," said Mey as he first looked into the object, then moved to look at the stars without it. "It's your turn, Treaia," Mey said, wanting to share what he saw with her.

"Everything becomes clearer and much larger when looking through this instrument. They are indeed wonderful, the things you have here in Nerius," Treaia said. "Look, there is one of those flying discs."

Everyone turned to look, as one of Nerius' flying craft circled in the air over the city. "Before long you will take a ride in one. We don't use them very often, since they seem to upset the people of the other lands. Zar will tell you more about the flying craft during your instruction," Tura told them.

The next day was the first of many, many months of instruction, most of which was given by Doctor Zar. They were so busy learning that they forgot to ask their questions about the great tower.

Their instructors and the rest of the people of Nerius were always helpful and friendly toward Mey and Treaia, but a student-teacher relationship was always maintained. This brought Mey and Treaia even closer in their friendship, and what little free time they had from their studies they spent together.

Weeks turned into months and the months became years as Mey and Treaia studied. Neither ever missed a class, not because they were ever commanded to attend, but because they wanted to learn. At last the thirst for true knowledge consumed them.

They learned the ways of the planets. They were taught to attune with all knowledge, both through books and through the use of their minds. The workings of machinery and solar energy were shown them, and many more wonderful things. They were so busy learning that they didn't have time yet to put to the test the things they had learned. Some afternoons were spent taking Kala for rides, so that he would not become lonely. Mey also took time, each day, to practice the bow as he had promised. They climbed the giant structure many times, each time with more fascination than before. One day, on approaching the tower, they thought they saw someone on the platform, but on reaching it, they found no one there.

"I have been meaning to ask you a question for a long time now," Mey addressed Doctor Zar one morning when there were no other students in the library but himself and Treaia. "Nebo said the tower was built by sounds of some sort. Do you really think that was possible?"

"Yes, it is very possible if one is trained. I will give you a demonstration, for it is one of the things you will learn while here in Nerius," Doctor Zar said, as he walked over to a shelf and took down a large book. Handing the book to Mey he said, "You and Treaia examine the book well, then take it to the back of the room."

Both Mey and Treaia examined the book thoroughly and placed it at the far end of the room; then they returned to where they could watch Doctor Zar closely.

Doctor Zar became very still. First with his eyes closed, then opening them wide, he began to make sounds, deep sounds that vibrated the air around him. The sounds became much like singing with the pitch rising up and down. Soon the book rose in the air, then it came toward Doctor Zar until it reached his open hand, which was extended with palm upward. There in the doctor's hand was the book he had called forth. He again handed them the book for further examination.

"That was wonderful to see," said Mey, for Treaia was still speechless.

"You will be taught this art, along with many other workings of nature's laws, in your studies," Doctor Zar said, as he smiled at them and went over to put his arm around their shoulders. "But I think today would be a good time to introduce you to the world of flying."

Leading the way, Doctor Zar took Mey and Treaia behind the building where they were taught about the stars. Here there was a large open space on which no vegetation grew. After walking over to a post that protruded from the ground, Doctor Zar made a strange adjustment to the post. The ground started spreading apart, and as it opened, a large disc, like the one they had seen in the air, rose up on a square platform, which stopped when it reached ground level. "Each new thing we see seems more wonderful than the last and yet equally magnificent," said Treaia, as they were being led to the disc.

"Ramana was taken to the temple in one of these when she was very small," Doctor Zar said, as he turned to Treaia.

They reached the craft, which was perfectly circular with windows covered by a clear substance all around. Doctor Zar held a door open for them to enter. "Take a seat, and put a strap across your lap. It will take a few minutes to get the craft ready," Doctor Zar directed, sitting down before a panel with many different buttons and lights. While pulling and pushing these lights and buttons, he talked to Treaia about Ramana.

"Ramana was chosen to serve the temple and you, by her stars. Before she was three years old she was sent to the temple. If she had stayed longer, it would have been too hard for her to leave Nerius. She was not able to go with her father and mother like Lasho did. I am very proud of the job she has done, for I loved her; she was my daughter." Zar looked lovingly at the child his daughter had been sent to raise.

"Thank you for letting her become my mother," Treaia said, smiling through her tears at Doctor Zar. "I do not understand how you knew I was to be raised by Ramana even before I was born. There was such a long time between Ramana's birth and mine."

"Our good King Nerius knows more about the stars than I. We were told of your coming even before Ramana was born. We knew of your coming also," Zar turned and looked at Mey.

"You keep speaking of our coming. I do not understand. I do not understand many things," Mey said in a questioning tone. "Did Lasho tell you?"

But Zar only said, "Here we go!" He seemed to be avoiding answering Mey.

The discussion was quickly forgotten in the thrill of rising high over the city. After circling and turning, they flew over the continent. "There is the village where Lasho and Hilo live," Doctor Zar said. "We will not fly very low, because it frightens people who do not know of our aircraft."

They flew over all the lands, with Doctor Zar telling

something about each one as they came to it. At last they were back over Nerius. Instead of landing, as Treaia and Mey had thought he would when they reached Nerius, Doctor Zar began taking the craft higher and higher. As he maneuvered the craft upward he said, "From the height we are attaining, you will be able to see the whole continent at once."

"It looks just like when I saw it in the crystal—like a heart," Mey said excitedly. "But it's so small from this height."

"The shape of the continent represents the love that is still to be learned on this planet," Doctor Zar said, as he looked down with them. "Would you like to take a long journey? If so, we will go around the globe, so that you might see this world we are on."

"Oh, yes," both answered, enthralled by the miracle that was happening to them.

"Love is a very advanced state," Doctor Zar continued, guiding the craft smoothly across the continent and out over the sea. "Almost a thousand years ago Nerius was settled. The race you see there was, and is still, the most advanced race on this planet. The people there have been taught for the past thousand years all the knowledge that is available on this planet. They are far advanced mentally, and now they are trying to learn perfect love. Those who come closest to this goal are sent off to serve, since only through active service can love be perfected. The wonders you have seen in Nerius will slowly be taught to the other lands as the people advance. The people of Nerius are the forerunners of this planet, yet perhaps only twenty have attained perfect love, as understood in this universe."

"Lasho told me that he has visions from his homeland giving him guidance," Treaia said, remembering the service Lasho gave his village.

"Yes, those that are sent out for service from Nerius are able to keep in contact mentally," answered Doctor Zar. "That is how Ramana knew she was to care for you. Ramana did not know from where she received her knowledge, only that it was for her to use. Ah, we have just begun crossing the largest continent on our planet. Even though it is larger, there are fewer inhabitants here."

Several hours were spent in traveling from one continent to another, over the islands and great seas. Doctor Zar explained about each land, the people from Nerius who were serving there, and what particular aspect of the whole was to be stressed. As they completed their journey and were circling Nerius for a landing, the sun made its way up over the horizon.

Mey and Treaia were dismissed from classes that day to rest. They were still too elated from the excitement of the trip to sleep, so they decided to take a walk to the cliff overlooking the beach where they had first been found by Tura and Nebo.

"Do you realize how long we've been in Nerius?" Treaia said as she looked down to the sea from the platform close to the lift. "These have been the most wonderful days of my life."

"Yes, and I at last fully realize something else," Mey said, as his face became serious. "You really are the girl of my dreams. You are the girl I saw in the crystal and I knew belonged to me. Why did it take so long?"

"Oh, my love," Treaia said, as she went into his arms. "I was just as blind when I was young. Now I am certain that you are the prince I was waiting for."

"Will you marry me, and become my queen?" asked Mey.

"With all my heart I want to be married to you and be your wife. To be your queen we would have to go to your kingdom. You don't want to leave Nerius, do you?"

"Let's not think of that now. I'm just happy to have really found you at last. We belong together like the sword and the jewels," he said as he held her close and kissed her.

Stepping back from their embrace, they saw the most superb rainbow either had ever seen, each color sparkling in its own brilliance. Neither questioned how there could be a rainbow on such a day.

Chapter Thirteen

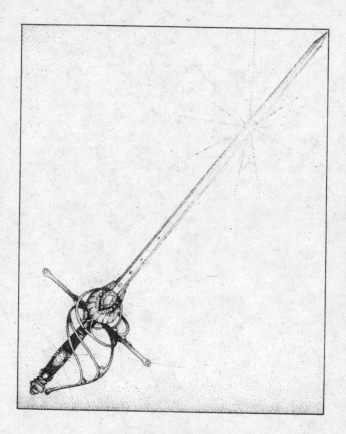

Nerius

As their knowledge grew, their love for each other became stronger and stronger. Mey's and Treaia's consciousness grew and expanded with each passing day of learning. As well as learning the laws and methods of this planet, they learned the ways of the stars in their universe.

One night after dinner, as they were walking by the fountain at the foot of the stairs, Treaia took Mey's hand and said, "We've been so happy in this marvelous city. Let's get married here and make Nerius our home. Oh, Mey, we could never have anything like this anywhere else."

"I have been thinking of the same thing, Treaia," Mey said, "but one thing bothers me. I promised my father to seek knowledge and then go home and teach the good that I found. At first I failed in so many things, I do not want to fail in this. But it would be nice if we could stay."

"No, you are right, knowledge found must be shared with others. We are blessed to have been able to learn here in Nerius. But what we have learned here is not needed here. We would be selfish to stay. Look at all the ones who belonged here in Nerius, yet they left this place of happiness to give to others. How can we do less?"

Both felt happy in their decision to go to Mey's land when the time came; they knew it was the right choice.

Walking hand in hand with Mey, Treaia said, "I had a dream about the tower last night, I'm sure there is a way inside."

"It's such a beautiful night. Why don't we go exploring—perhaps we can find it," Mey said, and holding Treaia's hand in his, he began walking in the direction of the giant tower.

Brilliant in its fullness, the moon shone down upon the tower, causing the gold in the quartz facing to sparkle like night fireflies. A sweet smell of fresh grass filled the air as they approached the most beautiful structure in Nerius.

"Remember how Nebo opened a door in the rock at the cliff? Perhaps there is an opening on one of these sides," Mey said, and he began to feel along the facing. Pushing and feeling, they searched all around the tower.

"Nothing, not even a hint of an opening," Treaia

155

said, sitting on the bottom step of the flight that led up to the tower platform.

"Do you suppose we both dreamed of a different structure?" pondered Mey as he joined her on the steps.

"Nebo said, as far as he knew, no one had ever entered it. Since we are here, shall we climb to the top and look at the stars?" asked Treaia.

Taking her hand and pulling Treaia to her feet was Mey's way of accepting her proposal. To climb to the platform on top of the tower was always exciting. Looking at the stars, magnified, thrilled them anew each time.

"Mey, look at the moon. I've never seen a rainbow around the moon before. Isn't it beautiful?" Treaia said, as she watched the colors completing a circle of splendor.

"Remember the day we saw the beautiful rainbow? Well, tonight we have a moonbow to share. That day at the lift, I felt I could never love more than that moment, but our love has grown even greater," Mey said, realizing that their love would become more and more complete as time went on. He bent down and kissed Treaia gently.

"We have grown in many ways since we began our journey, learned so many things. It will be hard to leave this wonderful kingdom," Treaia said, as they stood watching the moonbow arm-in-arm.

They turned from the wall, ready to leave, but then they stopped, rooted to the spot. The middle of the platform started lifting up like a trapdoor, and excitement surged through them as they watched the entrance open before them as if by magic. They did not hesitate for a moment, but rushed over to the opening and saw stairs leading down. Down, down they went, turning first one way then another until they were in the heart of the tower. Coming to a giant door, inset with jewels and symbols, they pushed on it, and it opened easily at the first touch, swinging wide to reveal the magnificence within.

"This is the room I dreamed of," Treaia said in a hushed voice.

Mey nodded in agreement, as he looked upward to a ceiling of majestic height. On the east wall, facing them, was an altar with fingers of golden light beaming down on a living flame that burned brightly from the center.

Gazing at the flame, Mey and Treaia began to feel dizzy. Their heads started spinning with the astonishing beauty they had found, and this spinning caused them to step outside of their physical bodies. Now they could see each other as they truly were—pure love. Looking at each other, they stepped toward one another and blended, becoming one.

"Well, done, my children, well done. You have quickly passed through all of this planet's trials, up to the highest point of attainment now possible here," Melk-edek's voice echoed in their ears, as they once again stepped inside their bodies. Turning to each other, they smiled with a golden radiance in their knowing of each other. Now they were truly one.

Looking again toward the altar, they saw a tall man of fair skin, with eyes like the sky on the clearest day. He was wearing a gold cordilier, like theirs, around his waist. He made a slight bow, and spoke with a voice full of love:

> "Hail, O keepers of the flame,
>   spreaders of light and truth,
> Joined with all the others
>   to work for the eternal youth.
> Hail, O keepers of the flame,
>   your strength comes from the sun;
> Because of your love for the Father
>   your hearts and minds are one.
> Hail, O keepers of the flame,
>   who will spend many years,
> Teaching all the others
>   to drive away the fears.
> Hail, O keepers of the flame,
>   the thirteenth did you ascend;
> Now you must help the others
>   to become the perfected ten.
> Hail, O keepers of the flame,
>   take out your jewels of light;
> Pull out the sword of power,
>   Now for the militant fight."

He walked toward them with arms outstretched in greeting. Only the love they had for each other surpassed what they instantly felt for this man. As he took their hands in his, he spoke again, saying, "You are manifesting as two flames, bearing the one flame of love."

Mey and Treaia bowed their heads as he held their hands, their eyes sparkling with tears of happiness.

"I am Nerius. It is now time to place the jewels within the sword," he said, as he held out his hands. Mey and Treaia undid the sword and the jewels from about their waists, and gave them to him. "At the highest step of learning, there must also be the highest step of uniting," smiled Nerius.

They watched Nerius solemnly set the stones in place. They realized that it would take time for them to understand the rush of visions coming to them as the dark veil was lifted during the ceremony. When the sword was again complete, Nerius faced Mey and Treaia, saying as he held the sword tenderly in his hands, "Having learned the ways and heartaches of the world has brought you the love, wisdom, and power of this sword. With the love that you have, now you are given the ability to wield all three—love, wisdom, and power—with authority." He placed the sword half in Treaia's hands and half in Mey's. He then gently guided them to the altar before the living flame and instructed them, "Place the sword of jewels here. One day another might find it. You are symbols of the sword and shall never lose what you have gained in seeking and finding its secret."

This done, Nerius led them out of the chamber. Soon they were once again standing on the platform of the tower, and there to greet them was Doctor Zar, smiling with the same tears of happiness. No one spoke as they all made their way down the stairs and into the city.

Going to meet Doctor Zar the next day for their usual morning instruction, they found not only the doctor but King Nerius as well. Mey and Treaia bowed low. Nerius came up to them and raised them up with his hands, saying, "Your studies are completed here, and it is time for you to return to the people of King Almar." Putting his arms around Mey and Treaia, he added solemnly, "You are embarking on your greatest adventure, using the knowledge you have acquired, and being living examples. Remember, this world's tomorrow begins with what you give it today. Let each new act be an act of improvement."

Epilogue

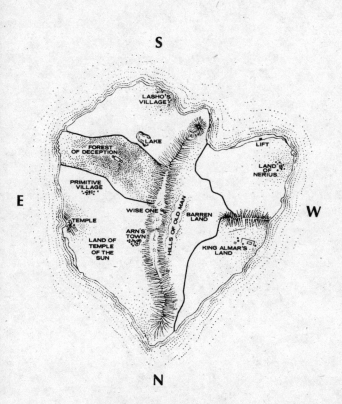

one continent on the
PLANET OF TEARS

The flying craft of Nerius had not been built to hold a horse the size of Kala. So when it was time to leave, a traveling party was arranged, made up of Nebo, Tura, and Doctor Zar, who were to escort Mey, Treaia, and Kala to the mountains that bordered the land of Nerius and the land of King Almar. There they were led as far down the mountains as possible, and lowered down the sheer face of the cliff in rope swings. Standing on the soil of the kingdom they were to rule, Mey and Treaia looked far above, where Nebo, Tura, and Doctor Zar were waving goodbye. It would be a long, long time before Mey and Treaia would see people like them again.

Mey and Treaia thought of the mountains many times, the high smooth stone that faced their land. Their kingdom was full of ignorance, but only a mountain away was all the knowledge in the world. A holiday was proclaimed on the day they were officially married and crowned king and queen before all the land. The people celebrated joyfully and were glad that their king had returned to rule them.

Now Mey and Treaia not only had each other, but since the ceremony in the tower, they could attune with Nerius and the others. They were also able to cross over the rainbow and visit their real home whenever they desired.

Mey and Treaia spent a long time touring the kingdom and getting to know more about the people. They wanted to share all their knowledge, but they found much resistance to new ideas. The people resisted any change, no matter how much it would benefit them, and they wanted things to stay the way they were. Mey and Treaia was saddened by this, since they had hoped, with all the knowledge they had acquired, that it would be easy to teach others. But they remembered that Lasho had said one step at a time. Yes, that was the only way. "That is the only way," the voice of Nerius whispered in their ears. "Go slowly. These people are not yet as you, and must be led slowly to learning. Be examples, for you together are wisdom and love. You symbolize the power and authority of the sword of jewels. By just being, you are living the right life. Some will notice and want to become like you. Others will go on resisting, so that they do not have to face up to themselves. But remember that what you give to them today, you will not see until another tomorrow."

Mey and Treaia worked hard at their life's task, and little by little they were successful. They felt that all of their own searching after knowledge had been worthwhile, since now they were able to pass some of it on to others, and be of service to their people. They knew that this was the highest goal. One day, when they were quite old, as they walked in the garden hand in hand, a golden wispy whirlwind came, and a soft voice whispered, "Well done, my children. Come home. Leave the Planet of Tears, until the next time comes to cross the rainbow bridge."

ABOUT THE AUTHOR

TRISH REINIUS, who has written both articles for national journals and television shows, was born in Bell, California. *The Planet of Tears* is her first fantasy novel. She has a wide range of interests which include music, metaphysics, yoga, karate, tennis, chess, drawing and painting. Trish Reinius now resides in Reno, Nevada.

ABOUT THE ILLUSTRATOR

BOB JOHNSON has contributed drawings and illustrations to more than twenty-five books. A resident of San Anselmo, California, Mr. Johnson is known for the lively satire of his often controversial, but always funny, cartoon strip which runs in *Funfinder Magazine*.